ATTACHMENT AND SEXUALITY
IN CLINICAL PRACTICE

The Centre for Attachment-based Psychoanalytic Psychotherapy

ATTACHMENT AND SEXUALITY IN CLINICAL PRACTICE

THE JOHN BOWLBY MEMORIAL CONFERENCE MONOGRAPH 2004

Edited by

Kate White

Published by
KARNAC

Published in 2005 by
Karnac (Books) Ltd.
6 Pembroke Buildings, London NW10 6RE

British Library Cataloguing in Publication Data

A C.I.P. for this book is available from the British Library

ISBN 1 85575 392 8

Edited, designed, and produced by The Studio Publishing Services Ltd, Exeter EX4 8JN

Printed in Great Britain by Hobbs the Printers Ltd

www.karnacbooks.com

CONTENTS

CONTRIBUTORS

Jody Messler Davies, PhD, is Co-editor of *Psychoanalytic Dialogues* and Faculty, Supervising Analyst, and former Co-chair of the Relational Track, New York University Postdoctoral Programme in Psychotherapy and Psychoanalysis. She has written many articles and is the author with M. G. Frawley (1994), of the book *Treating the Adult Survivor of Childhood Sexual Abuse: A Psychoanalytic Perspective.*

Bernice Laschinger had many years of experience in community mental health prior to becoming an attachment-based psychoanalytic psychotherapist. She is a member of CAPP, where she is a training therapist, teacher, and supervisor and has been very involved in the development of CAPP's training curriculum, particularly with the integration of the relational model of psychoanalysis into the course.

Joanna Ryan, PhD, is a psychoanalytic psychotherapist, supervisor and researcher. She trained at the Philadelphia Association and is currently a member of The Site for Contemporary Psychoanalysis. She has worked in voluntary organizations and in private practice. She is co-author (with Noreen O'Connor) of *Wild Desires and*

Mistaken Identities: Lesbianism and Psychoanalysis (reprinted by Karnac in 2003), and the author of *The Politics of Mental Handicap* (Free Association Books), as well as many other publications. She is currently conducting a research project on social class and psychotherapy.

Joseph Schwartz, PhD, is a training therapist and supervisor at CAPP. Originally trained as an experimental particle physicist, he worked for fifteen years in mental health research before becoming a clinician. His latest book is *Cassandra's Daughter: A History of Psychoanalysis in Europe and America*. (2003), London: Karnac.

Kate White is a training therapist, supervisor and teacher at the Centre for Attachment-based Psychoanalytic Psychotherapy. Formerly senior lecturer at South Bank University in the Department of Nursing and Community Health Studies, she has used her extensive experience in adult education to contribute to the innovative psychotherapy curriculum developed at CAPP. In addition to working as an individual psychotherapist, Kate runs workshops on the themes of attachment and trauma in clinical practice. One of her particular interests is in sibling relationships.

Rachel Wingfield has been Chair of CAPP since 2001. She trained at CAPP and is a training therapist, teacher and supervisor. She has experience in a wide range of clinical settings, including within institutions and the voluntary sector, and currently works as a psychotherapist in private practice, as well as in prisons. Rachel has a particular interest in working clinically with issues of sexuality, violence, and abuse.

Judy Yellin is a registered member of the Centre for Attachment-based Psychoanalytic Psychotherapy where she is a member of the teaching staff. She also has a legal background and provides training on the interface between psychotherapy, counselling and the law. Judy has a particular interest in questions of attachment, sexuality, and gender and working with lesbians, gay men, and transgendered clients from a relational perspective.

ACKNOWLEDGEMENTS

Thanks to the Bowlby Memorial Conference 2004 Planning Group: Wayne Barron, Sarah Benamer, Christine Blake, Richard Bowlby, Penny McMillan, Joseph Schwartz, Rachel Wingfield and Judy Yellin for their creative work in producing a stimulating and ground-breaking conference that has enabled the emergence of this exciting monograph. A special thank you to all the contributors to the conference whose innovative work can now reach a much wider audience.

Finally thanks to our eleventh John Bowlby Memorial Lecturer, Jody Messler Davies, for her lively and thought provoking presentation, around which this conference was planned.

A special thank you to Judy Yellin for her help in the editing process and to Leena Hakkinen at Karnac Books for her patience and support.

Kate White
December 2004

Attachment and sexuality in clinical practice

Introduction to the monograph of the John Bowlby Memorial Conference 2004

Kate White

T he significance of attachment and its relationship to sexuality is crucial in our psychological worlds. This collection of papers from the 11th John Bowlby Memorial Conference, *Attachment and Sexuality in Clinical Practice*, brings together the work of a group of outstanding clinicians and innovative thinkers in the field of attachment and relational psychoanalysis. Each paper is richly textured, weaving together the themes of attachment and sexuality, taking us from a wonderful historical overview through intricate theoretical pathways to vivid descriptions of how it feels to both analyst and analysand in the intensity of a therapeutic relationship.

Why does sexuality become the arena in which fundamental relational issues and struggles are played out? Mitchell (1988, p. 102) suggests that in part it is because of the connections of sexual desire to body sensations, and the echoes that these have with our early attachment relationships. It is perhaps how these experiences are registered in our bodies which has such an impact on our sexual relationships. As Susie Orbach suggests (2004, p. 28): *"There is . . . no such thing as a body, there is only a body in relationship with another body"*.

It seemed fitting to take the theme of last year's conference *Touch: Attachment and the Body*, and to extend the boundary of our discussion to the theme of attachment and sexuality in clinical practice as the focus for the conference in 2004.

As well as sexuality's link to our corporeality, expressions of our desire for intimacy, recognition, and connection infuse our sexual relating and can be used to communicate a whole range of emotions—love, reparation, conflict, anxiety, escape, passion, and rapture. In our efforts to overcome isolation, and following a desire to be known and to be seen, we risk the loss of privacy as well as the threat of the loss of an attachment so yearned for and yet so feared when we engage in intimate sexual relating. The links between attachment and sexuality are there, but are in need of further theorizing. That is what we set out to accomplish in putting on this conference, so these papers provide an exploration of attachment and sexuality within a relational matrix and the emergence of these themes in therapeutic work.

The first paper "'Such stuff as dreams are made on': sexuality as re/creation", by Judy Yellin, is an inspired introduction to the post-modern landscape in relation to gender and sexuality, and the role of culture in creating our embodied psychic realities. She asks the question "Can we reorient our psychoanalytic thinking so as to recreate our selves?" Her paper challenges us to explore, with greater openness in ourselves, the culture-bound categories of gender and sexuality. We are encouraged towards greater flexibility and fluidity in our thinking about our sexual and gender identity, and to think about how this impacts upon our relationships with clients.

Joanna Ryan's response explores and extends our thinking, arguing that any psychotherapy should incorporate a queer theory approach, since it relates to how experience, identity, subjectivity, and desire are lived and constructed within the context of language and differential power relations. She describes clinical vignettes that vividly illustrate the relevance of this argument to clinical practice.

Joseph Schwartz takes up the emergence in clinical practice of the links between attachment and sexuality. He describes an exploration with a group of colleagues of how themes of attachment and sexuality appeared in their work with clients. The unique difficulties involved in being able to explore openly sexual feelings in the therapeutic relationship, without closing them down prematurely, are discussed, and he outlines some theoretical implications of Fairbairn's understanding of mature dependency for male sexuality.

His paper set the scene for small group discussions at the conference and notes from these can be accessed on our website: www.attachment.org.uk, where there is also a review of the conference by Sarah Jack.

The Bowlby Memorial Lecture was given by Jody Messler Davies, co-editor of *Psychoanalytic Dialogues* and co-author of *Treating Adult Survivors of Child Sexual Abuse: A Psychoanalytic Perspective* (1994). Her paper, entitled "The times we sizzle, and the times we sigh: the multiple erotics of arousal, anticipation, and release", is a beautiful description of her work with seventy-five-year-old Rose. In this remarkable study of their relationship she weaves a richly textured account of their joint exploration of Rose's old and new love relationships and developing erotic sexual desire in the context of later life. Jody also considers whether an extension of Fairbairn's ideas about the exciting libidinal object may help to theorize the adult capacity for sexual pleasure as founded on the necessary developmental achievement of a capacity for pleasurable anticipation.

The final paper in this collection is a response to Jody Davis by Rachel Wingfield, Chair of the Centre for Attachment-based Psychoanalytic Psychotherapy. Rachel discusses Jody's presentation and further develops her theoretical proposal. She reminds us of the social and historical context of women's sexual desire within Western culture.

Rachel links secure attachment to a capacity for intersubjective and sustained intimacy, which she illustrates with a clinical vignette that is reminiscent of what Stern (1998) describes as a "moment of meeting". These moments are key to therapeutic change, the consequences of which are a move to a new level in the therapeutic relationship.

These themes linking attachment and sexuality are reiterated by Stephen Mitchell:

> Thus, sexuality plays a central role in most intimate relationships.
> . . . it is establishment and maintenance of relatedness that is

fundamental, and the mutual exchange of intense pleasure and emotional responsiveness is perhaps the most powerful medium in which emotional connection and intimacy is sought, established, lost and regained. [Mitchell, 1988, p. 107]

The range and depth of issues addressed by the contributors to this volume, writing from an attachment and relational perspective, present a well argued and inspiring set of papers for us to study.

References

Davies, J. M., & Frawley, M. G. (1994). *Treating the Adult Survivor of Childhood Sexual Abuse: A Psychoanalytic Perspective.* New York: Basic Books.

Mitchell, S. A. (1988). Sex without drive (theory). In: S. A. Mitchell (Ed.), *Relational Concepts in Psychoanalysis* (pp. 94–122). Cambridge, MA: Harvard University Press.

Orbach, S. (2004). The body in clinical practice. Part One: There is no such thing as a body. In: K. White (Ed.), *Touch, Attachment and the Body.* London: Karnac.

Stern, D., Sander, L. W., Nahum, J. P., Harrison, A. M., Lyons-Ruth, K., Morgan, A. C., Bruschweiller-Stern, N., & Tronick, E. Z. (1998). Non-interpretive mechanisms in psychoanalytic therapy, The "something more" than interpretation. *International Journal of Psycho-Analysis, 79*: 903–911.

Attachment theory and the John Bowlby Memorial Lecture

A short history

Bernice Laschinger

The theme of this year's Bowlby lecture marks the movement within attachment theory towards the integration of sexuality in its theory and clinical practice. Sexuality was not a focus of theoretical concern for Bowlby. He emphasized that attachment was a motivational system in its own right, separate from sexuality and feeding. Like other relational theories, attachment theory has been criticized for its failure to theorize these areas. However, recently it has come to be understood that attachment is a bodily experience; it has always been implicit in the basic premise of the child's need for proximity to the body of the mother. This recognition has, in turn, highlighted the child's sensual bond with the mother in influencing adult patterns of sexuality. Indeed, within contemporary relational theories, sexuality has come to be seen as the central arena in which the dramas of attachment are played out—in which "emotional connection and intimacy is sought, established, lost and regained" (Mitchell, 1988, p. 107).

These themes, thus, link to the origins of attachment theory. As a teacher of deprived children and later as a child psychiatrist, Bowlby became powerfully aware of the longing of young children for the physical presence of their care-givers and of their

5

corresponding traumatic experiences of separation and loss. These perceptions laid the empirical foundations of the theory.

Bowlby's post-war studies of refugee children led to the publication of his seminal work, *Maternal Care and Mental Health* by the World Health Organization in 1952. He also studied children in hospital and a residential nursery, in conjunction with James Robertson, who filmed them. The documented sequence of the children's responses to separation in terms of protest, detachment, and despair provided evidence of separation anxiety. The impact of these ideas on the development of child care policy has been enormous. The 2001 Bowlby Lecturer, Michael Rutter, discussed institutional care and the role of the state in promoting recovery from neglect and abuse. His lecture was a testament to the continuing relevance of Bowlby's thinking to contemporary social issues.

Although Bowlby joined the British Psychoanalytic Society in the 1930s and received his training from Joan Riviere and Melanie Klein, he became increasingly sceptical of their focus on the inner fantasy life of the child rather than real life experience, and tended towards what would now be termed a relational approach. Thus, in searching for a theory that could explain the anger and distress of separated young children, Bowlby turned to disciplines outside psychoanalysis, such as ethology. He became convinced of the relevance of animal, and particularly primate, behaviour to our understanding of the normal process of attachment. These relational concepts presented a serious challenge to the closed world of psychoanalysis in the 1940s, and earned Bowlby the hostility of his erstwhile colleagues for several decades.

The maintenance of physical proximity by a young animal to a preferred adult is found in a number of animal species. This suggested to Bowlby that attachment behaviour has a survival value, the most likely function of which is that of care and protection, particularly from predators. It is activated by conditions such as sickness, fear, and fatigue. Threat of loss leads to anxiety and anger; actual loss to anger and sorrow. When efforts to restore the bond fail, attachment behaviour may diminish, but will persist at an unconscious level and may become reactivated by reminders of the lost adult, or new experiences of loss.

Attachment theory's basic premise is that, from the beginning of life, the baby human has a primary need to establish an emotional bond with a care-giving adult. Attachment is seen as a source of human motivation as fundamental as those of food and sex. Bowlby postulated that

Attachment behaviour is any form of behaviour that results in a person attaining or maintaining proximity to some other preferred and differentiated individual . . . While especially evident during early childhood, attachment behaviour is held to characterise human beings from the cradle to the grave. [Bowlby, 1979, p. 129]

Attachment theory highlights the importance of mourning in relation to trauma and loss. An understanding of the relevance of this to therapeutic practice was a vital element in the foundation of the Centre for Attachment-based Psychoanalytic Psychotherapy (CAPP). The consequences of disturbed and unresolved mourning processes was a theme taken up by Colin Murray Parkes when he gave the first John Bowlby Memorial Lecture.

Mary Ainsworth, an American psychologist who became Bowlby's lifelong collaborator, established the interconnectedness between attachment behaviour, care-giving in the adult, and exploration in the child. While the child's need to explore, and the need for proximity might seem contradictory, they are in fact complementary. It is the mother's provision of a secure base, to which the child can return after exploration, that enables the development of self-reliance and autonomy. Ainsworth developed the "Strange Situation Test" for studying individual differences in the attachment patterns of young children. She was able to correlate these to their mothers' availability and responsiveness. Her work provided both attachment theory and psychoanalysis with empirical support for some basic premises. This established the necessary link between attachment concepts and their application to individual experience in a clinical setting.

Over the last two decades the perspective of attachment theory has been greatly extended by the work of Mary Main, who was another Bowlby Lecturer. She developed the "Adult Attachment Interview" in order to study the unconscious processes that underlie the behavioural pattern of attachment identified by Mary Ainsworth. Further support came from the perspective of infant observation and developmental psychology developed by yet another Bowlby Lecturer, Daniel Stern. The Bowlby Lecturer for 2000, Allan Schore, presented important developments in the new field of neuro-psychoanalysis, describing emerging theories of how attachment experiences in early life shape the developing brain.

The links beween attachment theory and psychoanalysis have also been developed. Jo Klein, a great supporter of CAPP and also a former contributor to the Bowlby Conference, has explored these links in psychotherapeutic practice. In particular, the 1998 Bowlby Lecturer, Stephen Mitchell, has identified a paradigm shift away from drive theory within psychoanalysis. His proposed "relational matrix" links attachment theory to other relational psychoanalytic theories that find so much resonance in the current social and cultural climate. Within this area of convergence, between attachment research and developmental psychoanalysis, the 1999 Bowlby Lecturer, Peter Fonagy, has developed the concept of "mentalization", extending our understanding of the importance of the reflective function, particularly in adversity.

In similar vein, the work of Beatrice Beebe, the 2001 Bowlby Lecturer, represents another highly creative development in the unfolding relational narrative of the researcher–clinician dialogue. Her unique research has demonstrated how the parent–infant interaction creates a distinct system organized by mutual influence and regulation, which are reproduced in the adult therapeutic relationship.

In the movement to bring the body into the forefront of relational theory and practice, last year's Bowlby Lecturer, Susie Orbach, a CAPP Trustee, has been a leading pioneer. It was the publication of her ground-breaking books, *Fat is a Feminist Issue* and *Hunger Strike*, that introduced a powerful and influential approach to the study of the body in in its social context. Over the last decade, one of her major interests has been the construction of sexuality and bodily experience in the therapeutic relationship.

Within this ground-breaking tradition, this year's Bowlby lecturer, Jody Messler Davies, who is co-editor of *Psychoanalytic Dialogues*, has made seminal contributions to the shaping of the American relational model. Her highly influential book, which she co-authored with Mary Gail Frawley, *Treating the Adult Survivor of Sexual Abuse* (1994), was a pioneering integration of trauma theory and relational psychoanalysis in the treatment of sexual abuse. Their conceptualization of transference–counter-transference as the vehicle for expressing dissociated traumatic experience was one of the first clinical applications of this relational approach. Since then she has extended these concepts in her original exploration of the erotic dimension of the therapeutic relationship and in her courageous development of the transformative uses of counter-transference disclosure.

References

Bowlby, J. (1952). *Maternal Care and Mental Health*, 2nd edn, World Health Organisation: Monograph Series, No. 2. Geneva: World Health Organisation.

Bowlby, J. (1979). *The Making and Breaking of Affectional Bonds*. London: Tavistock.

Davies, J. M., & Frawley, M. G. (1994). *Treating the Adult Survivor of Childhood Sexual Abuse: A Psychoanalytic Perspective*. New York: Basic Books.

Mitchell, S. A. (1988). Sex without drive (theory). In: S. A. Mitchell (Ed.), *Relational Concepts in Psychoanalysis* (pp. 94–122). Cambridge, MA: Harvard University Press.

"Such stuff as dreams are made on": sexuality as re/creation

Judy Yellin

"Mapping the territory?"

As a member of the Centre for Attachment-based Psycho-analytic Psychotherapy's planning group for this Bowlby Memorial Conference of 2004, I have been charged by my colleagues with the awesome responsibility of "mapping the territory" of contemporary relational psychoanalytic thinking about sexuality and attachment. The mapping of this territory, it seems to me, is a very tricky business, particularly where that territory is as vast, complex, and strongly contested as that of sexuality.

So which territory am I to talk about exactly? Where is it and how do we get there? How does it take its shape, how large an area am I to try to explore, where am I to perceive its borders to be? Are sexuality and attachment one territory, in any case? Should they be? Or are they two separate territories, with different terrains, cultures, languages? If so, do they adjoin or are there disputed border areas between them?

Given that sexualities are expressed through and in the territory of bodies, how are these bodies constructed, how do they come about? What do they feel like when we experience them as "feeling sexual?" Does the way they look to the outside bear any relation to the way they feel on the inside? Should it? Are men's bodies always male, masculine? Are women's always female, feminine? What do we mean by "men" and "women" anyway? When we desire, who are we? And who or what do we desire? Is our desire always and inevitably gendered? Can we imagine our desire in a different gender? Without gender? What would this mean?

And at what co-ordinates do I locate myself in setting out on such an exercise? It seems I need to orient myself first, so it's clear where my starting point is. After all, orientation is clearly of more than passing interest in a survey of the contemporary sexual land-scape. My perspective will inevitably be grounded in my own previous explorations of the terrain—where I've been, the route I took to get there, who I met on the way. I know some parts of the terrain better than others, and my map will look quite different from a map drawn by someone with another point of departure. I'll try to explain.

What is this thing called "queer"?

In attempting to establish a suitable orientation point for this paper I found myself thinking about Freud's (1905d) "Three essays on the theory of sexuality". It struck me that we are today almost exactly one hundred years from its publication in 1905, and I was momen-tarily captured by the idea that this would provide a neat spring-board from which to dive into contemporary psychoanalytic waters and see where we are now, a century on from one of Freud's most innovative and defining texts on the "nature" of sexuality.

But within seconds of my first thought about a century of psychoanalytic sexual theory, I was deflated by a second thought. After all, we are now only in the year 2004, and the "Three essays" will not have their centenary until next year—so a neat statement about "one hundred years of sexual theorizing" couldn't actually work. We still have a year to go, and "Ninety-nine years of sexual theorizing" simply doesn't have the same symmetry or resonance to it. Only "one hundred" conveys an interval of years worthy of reference, imbued with significance, a cultural landmark. Ninety-nine years just misses that mark. For these purposes, it's a defective number. I was genuinely disturbed and frustrated by this discrepancy of a year, and I thought I'd better drop the idea and start again.

But then it occurred to me that the number 100, with its powerful associations of meaningful historical value, is purely arbitrary, a norm plucked from infinite numerical possibilities within a variety of possible counting systems. The shared social significance of using a base of ten in our particular system simply freights some numbers with a heavy symbolic load, in this instance to such an extent that I felt hampered in what I could meaningfully say by the deficit of one year.

Why am I telling you this? Not simply to acknowledge that talking about or writing about sexuality is bound to arouse anxiety. I'm telling you because I realized that I was inflicting a mental operation on myself that illustrates precisely the problematic of our culture in relation to sexuality and gender, as in relation to so many other aspects of our subjectivities. In relation to 100, ninety-nine isn't just an odd number, it's a *queer* number. It's queer not only in its original Old High German sense of "off-centre", "perverse", "odd", but also in the sense meant by what we have come to know as "queer theory", a way of looking at the world according to which: "Queer is by definition whatever is at odds with the normal, the legitimate, the dominant . . .". (Halperin, quoted in Gauntlett, 1998)

"Queer" also, of course, appears in the dictionary, from at least 1922 onwards, as a pejorative adjective meaning "homosexual". Its reclamation began with lesbian and gay political activism in the 1980s. But now the ideas of "queer" theory can be found throughout cultural and gender studies, most particularly under the umbrella of what have come to be called "post-modern" or "post-structuralist" or "post-colonialist" accounts of subjectivity—of how we come to experience ourselves as we do, and to claim the identities we claim. "Queer" may have begun as a critique of heteronormativity—"all those ways in which the world makes sense from a heterosexual point of view" and which "assumes that a complementary relation between the sexes is both a natural arrangement (the ways things are) and a cultural ideal (the way things should be)" (Dean, 2003, p. 238). But now it no longer simply refers to sexual and gender presentations that transgress norms, but to a "way of seeing" (Berger, 1972) that identifies and challenges normative structures of all kinds and tries to open up our minds to new ways of imagining ourselves that are less bound by old, invisible assumptions. This definition of queer theory may produce a *déjà vu* for psychoanalytic practitioners. To parody the words of the Hollywood disclaimer: any similarity to any theory, living or dead, is entirely intentional.

Queers in space

In thinking about sexuality and attachment within the territory of our consulting rooms, relational psychoanalysis is increasingly calling upon queer and post-modernist perspectives flourishing in other territories—vibrant and challenging debates that have been taking place in the worlds of literary and cultural criticism, philosophy and sociology, feminist theory, and lesbian and gay studies. Common ground is being established. New perspectives are emerging, which acknowledge how each of our unique subjectivities come about within a matrix of interconnecting and conflicting social forces.

The cartographers of sexuality within psychoanalysis are no longer a monopoly of mapmakers who locate the centre of the sexual territory at the spot where they happen to be standing. If psychoanalysis once resembled a pre-Copernican universe, with heterosexual procreative genital sex at its centre, a contemporary psychoanalytic astronomy re-orientates the map, de-centres it, and suggests the possibility of many different centres. We may find that the further we travel from the dense mass of established cultural and psychoanalytic "truths"—about sexuality, about gender—the less we are subject to its gravitational force. We may feel as if we are becoming disorientated. If we want to explore in space, we may have to get used to being gravity-free and letting ourselves—and our minds—float, at least temporarily.

The (queer) repressed returns to Freud

So, bearing all this in mind, I want to return to the "queer" observation that Freud's "Three essays" was published ninety-nine years ago. Why should we still care what Freud had to say about sex and gender so long ago, in an era of European history surely so much less tolerant than our own? Surely we are now more accepting of diversity, less pathologizing of difference? As Robert May asks in an essay on re-reading Freud on homosexuality:

> Why bother reading Freud? I gather it is possible to be interested in psychoanalysis these days without reading Freud. Perhaps it is also possible to be a philosopher without reading Plato. [May, 1995, p. 156]

I would like to adopt May's own answer to this question:

> Psychoanalysis remains lively in part because Freud's writing is so full of complexity, layering and contradiction that it not only allows but *requires* rereading from different points of view. [*ibid.*]

This contradictory character of Freud's seems to lie at the heart of the "Three essays", and his account of gender and sexuality generally. It is as if there are two Freuds at work in the text—Freud the radical and Freud the conservative—each ambivalently challenging and destabilizing the other. Freud the radical *breaks up*—we would now say that he *deconstructs*—the monolithic conventional understanding of how sexuality is put together. Freud treats sexuality like a jigsaw puzzle, and separates it out into various component pieces—bodies, sexes, genders, aims, and objects. He rejects any equivalence between sexuality and heterosexuality, and apparently severs the links between what we call "sexual orientation" and what we call "gender identity". This lets him—and us—play with the jigsaw puzzle pieces into which unitary sexuality has been broken apart.

But although Freud the radical broke the jigsaw puzzle up into pieces, Freud the conservative then set about putting them back together to try to remake the picture on the front of the box—that picture of the "normal" heterosexual couple having procreative genital sex. His radical theory of sexuality ran side by side with a developmental theory of sexuality, pointing towards a stage of maturity, of completion. Of course, a theory with a goal, a desired end point, is always a theory imbued with values. Even, or rather, especially, where those values seem so self-evident as the values of "nature", "biology", and "reproduction of the species". That makes psychoanalysis, inevitably, a political theory—an ideology as well as a treatment.

There were limits to how far Freud was able or prepared to go in questioning why, for instance, the jigsaw pieces had just those particular shapes in the first place—the active and passive shapes, masculine and feminine shapes, penis and vagina shapes, boy and girl shapes—and why it always seemed that the shapes had to come in opposing pairs. The fact that the pieces come in particular shapes suggests that the jigsaw can only be put together neatly in one particular way—active fits with masculine, fits with penis, fits with boy; and passive fits with feminine, fits with vagina, fits with girl. To try to make a different picture means forcing pieces in where they don't belong, or, worse, cutting the corners off some and adding bits to others—alternative pictures of sexuality can only be created either by a "castration" or by a "phoney" addition of some kind.

The "queer" underpinning of psychoanalysis, with its project of recognizing and reintegrating the excluded, the disavowed and the repressed, particularly in the arena of sexual life, is what made it a theory with revolutionary potential. In the process of becoming a "professional science" though, the danger is that reintegration somehow becomes assimilation. The unsettling insights of psycho-analysis get re-repressed. Rather than transformation, we settle for conformation. Did psychoanalysis somehow lose its queerness, become respectable, learn to pass as straight? Post-modern theorists are now seeking to re-queer psychoanalysis.

The structure of psychoanalytic revolutions

In 1962 Thomas Kuhn's classic, *The Structure of Scientific Revolutions*, provided a pithy description of how our fundamental models for understanding the world get established, and how, by way of revo-lutionary shifts in perception, each model is successively replaced by new models, the old models gradually fading away. When a persistent anomaly can no longer be ignored by, or subsumed within, existing shared assumptions about the world, a scientific "crisis" occurs, which may lead to a paradigm shift (Kuhn, 1962).

We could see the "Three essays" as a microcosm of such a scien-tific crisis—of a struggle between two paradigms. The old model of sexuality sees our sexual subjectivities as ultimately shaped by a biological, reproductive imperative, which is expressed by self-evidently physically sexed bodies. Any variations represent developmental failures on the part of the organism. The new model sees human sexuality as constructed purely out of our relations with each other—polymorphous, without any preordained form and, for Freud, uncertain in its aims and purpose, apart from the notion of pleasure.

Alongside Freud's frequent appeals to "constitution"—his code word for innate biological predispositions—are his equally frequent appeals to "the accidental", the cultural, the anthropological. When he refers to sexual customs in ancient Greek society or to the anthropology of homosexuality, Freud isn't appealing to biology as the foundation for variation in sexual practices. He is clearly talking about culture, about what we now call the "social construction" of sexuality. Freud's radical sexual theory repeatedly shows us that masculinity and femininity, together with homosexual and heterosexual object choices, are not inborn. They are achievements, and precarious achievements, born of disappointments and threats, at that.

We begin to get a sense of the revolutionary potential of his views when radical Freud makes the revolutionary statement:

> Psychoanalytic research is most decidedly opposed to any attempt at separating off homosexuals from the rest of mankind as a group of special character . . . it has found that all human beings are capable of making a homosexual object-choice and have in fact made one in their unconscious . . . psychoanalysis considers that a choice of an object independently of its sex—freedom to range equally over male and female objects—. . . is the original basis from which, as a result of restriction in one direction or another, both the normal and inverted types develop. *Thus from the point of view of psychoanalysis the exclusive sexual interest felt by men for women is also a problem that needs elucidating and is not a self-evident fact based upon an attraction that is ultimately of a chemical nature.* [Freud, 1905d, my italics]

But the promise held out here was not subsequently followed up by psychoanalysis as a treatment, as a theory, or as a training. Instead of an exploration and a challenge, the "problem" of heterosexuality became a compulsory developmental schema and a set of prescriptions. The problem for psychoanalysis after Freud became not how to question heterosexuality, but how to inculcate it—how to go back down the developmental path and retrieve the dawdling childish libidos of inverts and perverts, so they could be persuaded and cajoled—dragged if necessary—towards the goal of proper grown-up sex.

Kuhn (1962) illustrated how we actually *see* different things under the influence of different paradigms by referring to the famous gestalt diagram of the duck and the rabbit—"what were ducks in the scientist's world before the revolution are rabbits afterward" (Figure 1). But Kuhn warns us that a genuine paradigm change doesn't simply involve being able to switch at will between alternative ways of seeing the same phenomenon. It involves seeing something entirely differently, and realizing that what we thought we saw before was never, in fact, a duck but was always, in fact, the rabbit. Freud couldn't decide if sexuality was a duck or a rabbit—and most psychoanalysts who came after him stuck with the biological, heteronormative duck and closed their eyes to the polymorphous, socially constructed rabbit. If there is now to be a paradigm change in psychoanalysis, we have to take the duck off the menu.

Duck is definitely off the menu in queer psychoanalysis.

What is this post-modernity?

"Post-modernism" sometimes just appears to be some trendy species of nihilism that proclaims that nothing means anything, everything is relative, there is no such thing as "truth". Or else it's a code word for theories so dense and abstruse that no one outside an ivory tower understands them, or even wants to try.

Figure 1

Modernism, we might say, is a cultural outlook that celebrates certainty and progress. It is on a quest to come closer and closer to some universal theory that will finally explain us to ourselves in a way that we can objectively know. It aims to hunt down that elusive and contested creature—"human nature"—once and for all, and tell us who we really are and should be. Often this is achieved by attributing some human characteristic to biology and genes, so that locating something within the body marks it as part of some internal, unchangeable essence of being human. It sets the limits of what we are able—or permitted—to think. Sex is such a category. Maleness and femaleness are seen as inevitable distinctions literally built into the morphology of our bodies, constructed from flesh, hormones, and chromosomes—material and, therefore, undeniable. This is *essentialism*, and it usually appeals to biology, as Freud appealed to "constitution". But the same effect can be achieved by citing culture rather than biology. For example, gender identity flows from sex—the sexed body is seen as the biological foundation, and the social gender is built on top of it. The shape of the architecture varies according to social norms, so that different gender possibilities are generated in different societies. But, at the end of the day, gender is fixed just as firmly in the mind by culture as sex is fixed in the body by nature. If it's not, then you're in big trouble and, as far as modernist psychoanalysis is concerned, you're probably a psychotic, or at any rate, a pervert, and you need help.

Post-modernisms question what we thought we knew to be true, and undermine the very foundations on which we and our clients stand—the apparently solid ground of our most hard-won achievement: our personal identity, our self. The post-modern self is divided, multiple, unstable, fluid, dissolving. It has difficulty holding on to a coherent vision of itself. Actually, it's not even trying. It celebrates this plurality and instability.

For post-modernists, the coherent self—including the sexed and gendered self—is a mere fiction. Many such theorists take their psychoanalytic inspiration from Lacan's (1966) re-reading of Freud, in which the coherent ego is an imaginary structure rather like a reel of film in which the gaps between frames go unnoticed, giving the impression of a continuity, but in fact relying on a continuous process of elision. This is difficult territory for us as relational psychotherapists because, as Lynne Layton (1998, p. 126) points out, what post-modernisms celebrate in theory, our clients experience as a source of torment in the clinic. Do these ideas, then, have anything positive to offer psychotherapists? Or are they more likely to be destructive and unhelpful in the consulting room? And what do they have to do with sex?

In their important book of essays about the developing relationship between relational psychoanalysis and post-modernism, Fairfield, Layton, and Stack (2002), remind us of Freud's ironic remark to Jung about psychoanalysis as they travelled to the USA in 1909. "Little do the Americans know", he said, "that we are bringing the plague." Fairfield, Layton, and Stack (2002, p.1) suggest that the arrival of post-modernity in psychoanalysis is perhaps the second plague.

As Fairfield says:

> [Postmodernism] is . . . what you get when a non-naïve modernity psychoanalyses itself. Can we go on to ask what it would be like for a non-naïve psychoanalysis to psychoanalyse itself, to address the tensions between modernism and post-modernism in its own theory and practice? [Fairfield, 2002, p. 70]

Perhaps we must inevitably regard it as a plague when we are required to deconstruct our foundational concepts and beliefs. But there are excitements and rewards for a psychoanalysis that can risk psychoanalysing itself, even if the process of such an analysis inevitably brings with it the anxieties that always accompany any process of change. Some of the foundational psychoanalytic signifiers of gender—the girl's wish for a penis, the boy's terror of castration—concepts Freud called the psychological "bedrock", springing from biological realities and thus beyond the reach of analytic change (Freud, 1937c)—might be re-opened. Their unconscious roots could be exposed, and their embeddedness in a specific *discourse* of gender and sexuality acknowledged.

And what is the Matrix?

The philosopher Slavoj Zizek (1999) has suggested that the movie *The Matrix* (Warner Brothers, 1999) functions like a Rorschach test, and in that spirit I've chosen to use it to illustrate the notion of gender discourse, specifically.

Liberated from his dream-like existence in the computer-generated false reality of the Matrix by a mysterious underground resistance, our hero Neo is inducted into the workings of the programme by his mentor, the underground leader Morpheus—who is named, appropriately enough, for the ancient Greek god, the "shaper" of dreams. Within the Matrix, Morpheus explains, external "reality" is "constructed" in line with whatever programme has been loaded. Even how we appear to ourselves and others reflects our "residual self-image"—a mental projection of a digital self. Reality itself is a desert, a post-apocalyptic shattered landscape—the "Desert of the Real"—which, the film suggests, exists unapprehended behind or beyond the dream-like construction in which we are immersed.

This paradoxical notion of false yet profoundly convincing and concretely experienced realities is taken up by post-modern accounts of subjectivity: accounts that draw heavily on Michel Foucault's idea of "discourse" (Foucault, 1978) and that seek to explain how we come to experience ourselves as the persons we feel ourselves to be and to adopt a variety of personal identities—male, female, gay, straight, black, white. "Discourses" are not only the ways we think and talk about the world; they are ways of organizing what we know, institutionally, socially and psychically; and the ways in which what we know "organizes" us. The power of a discourse is that it does not simply *describe* a state of affairs; it actually *produces* it. It creates, and recreates, that state of affairs. Discourses bring us—their subjects—into being, including our psychic and *physical* being.

"Physical being" is not simply the materiality of our bodies—the apparently irreducible biological "facts" of cells, blood, flesh—but the *lived experience* of that materiality. It is the *psychic reality* of inhabiting that flesh, that blood which is moulded by discourse, which produces the internal conviction, for example, of being a "man", a "woman", the experience of inhabiting a body that feels itself to be sexed "male" or "female". Materiality itself, outside of any discourse, simply has no intrinsic meaning, and thus cannot be thought or spoken about at all. This unthinkable, meaningless materiality is what is known in Lacanian parlance as "the Real", the closest a human being can ever get to such a thing as a state of "nature".

As psychotherapists interested in attachment and its traumatic failures, we come to know well in our clinical work the consequences of the unspeakable and unsymbolized for our own and our clients' senses of our own embodiment. Dissociation is often precisely an experience of being disembodied, out of body, of physical non-existence. If our immersion in the relational matrix can make us feel as if we have no bodies at all, then it can also make us feel as if we have the bodies of boys and girls, men and women, in whatever ways our version of the matrix makes those experiences "experienceable".

As Lynne Layton has noted, the discourse of sex and gender in our culture:

> ... dictates what kinds of minds and bodies are speakable, what kinds unspeakable; what parts of the body are sanctioned as erogenous zones, what parts are not; what counts as a gender identity and what does not; and which sexual practices have legitimacy and which do not. [Layton, 1998, p. 9]

Our culture prizes very highly the idea that we should always feel ourselves to be essentially the same person, and that we should achieve a stable personal identity. This stability is often central to ideas of psychological and emotional health. Nowhere is this more desirable than in the area of sexuality and gender. Not to be certain of our gender, and how to behave in a manner "appropriate" to it; or not to be sure of our sexual orientation, and how to organize our relationships around it, can have serious consequences for our social and emotional lives. It provokes enormous amounts of anxiety, in ourselves and others. We may therefore tend to scramble for a coherent identity, and then cling on to it for dear life.

Q: How many post-modernists does it take to change a binary? A: The more the better!

Our particular sexual discourse, the way that we structure how it is possible for us to think about ourselves, works on the principle of Noah's Ark in every area of our experience: things come in sets of two, in binaries. If we *count* on a base of ten, we tend to *think* on a base of two. The Cartesian discourse of binary opposites is the invisible and ubiquitous organizer of our minds. Even the use of the word "mind" participates in the binary split—the missing term, of course, is "body". This split thinking is an unconscious process, embedded in language. We don't even know we're doing it, and when it's pointed out to us, it can feel as though basic common sense, or our very reality, is being questioned.

Descartes didn't invent dualism, of course—it's been with us for thousands of years. Among countless others, dualism gives us some of our most powerful organizing principles: male and female; masculine and feminine; active and passive; subject and object; heterosexual and homosexual; rich and poor; white and black; adult and child; mature and immature; healthy and sick; normal and perverse; good and evil; Eros and Thanatos.

Neither one of each pair can stand alone—its definition depends upon its opposite number. Nor are these terms on *equal* terms. They are always asymmetrically, hierarchically related—the first term of the duo always appearing as "superior", more powerful, than the second. So we know what masculine is only because it's not feminine and vice versa. What's active is defined by what it's not—passive. Each term excludes the qualities contained in its opposite number, and can only maintain its existence by ensuring that it remains uncontaminated by what it repudiates. Thus, for Freud (1925j), "masturbation (in women), at all events of the clitoris, is a masculine activity and the elimination of clitoridal sexuality is a necessary precondition for the development of femininity".

At the same time, an identity based upon a rigid binary category is always unstable, brittle, illusory. It is always undermined from without by what it attempts to exclude, and from within by what it attempts to repress. Any close analysis of one side of a supposedly stable binary quickly starts to break down, as its indebtedness to the other side of the equation betrays its hybrid nature. Where does feminine end and masculine begin? Most of us exist in this hybrid state in which we are each continually constructing our own alloys of self from identifications drawn from each side of the binary divide. Nevertheless, the socially constructed reality in which we live out our identities remains organized along binary principles, so that we must repeatedly, and largely unconsciously, renegotiate the tensions between compliance with binary norms and resistance to them. This may mean, for example, that we never actually feel secure in our identities as masculine or feminine, but depend rather upon creating a "good enough" impression of our gender, a "masquerade", the "naturalness" of which may feel intermittent. We may feel that we are "passing", some or all of the time.

It's about power . . .

Why are we so in thrall to these wounding cultural norms, even when compliance with them can profoundly constrict our human possibilities? And why is it so hard to change them? In the discourse of early attachment, adult carers exercise power by deploying love. Caught in the binary tension between attachment needs and resistance to norms, attachment often wins out (Layton, 1998, p. 231). We disavow our possibilities rather than lose love or incur social shame.

We are all entangled in matrices woven from the ley lines of different binary discourses. The complex and contradictory distributions of power created by different discourses can allow us to experience ourselves as both relatively power*ful* and power*less*. It just depends on where we're standing and how power lines intersect at that spot. We then make choices about whether and how to deploy whatever power is available to us to exercise.

Angels in America does Foucault

In Tony Kushner's *Angels in America* (Kushner, 1992; Nichols, 2003), Roy Cohn, closeted homosexual, right-wing Republican power-broker, whose influence extends not merely to the President of the United States but, far more potently, to his wife, knows that it is how we are *named*, how we are *located* in discourse, that dictates where we will be positioned in the hierarchy of power. Diagnosed with AIDS by Henry, his old friend and doctor for the last thirty years, Roy will not permit Henry to speak aloud the words that, if applied to him, would instantaneously strip him of the power and privilege he has spent a lifetime pursuing.

Roy: ...You know, your problem, Henry, is that you are hung up on *words*. On labels, that you believe that they mean what they seem to mean. AIDS, homosexual, gay, lesbian. You think these are names that tell you who someone sleeps with? They don't tell you that.

Henry: No?

Roy: No! Like all labels, they tell you one thing, one thing only. Where does an individual so identified fit in the food chain? In the pecking order. Not ideology, or sexual taste, but something much simpler. Clout.

And so, he is not a "homosexual"—since within the dominant discourse homosexuals are by definition men without power, without clout. He does not have AIDS—the disease of the powerless faggot male—but liver cancer. Because Roy *has* power, *has* clout, and plenty of it. As he succinctly puts it: "Because *what* I am is defined entirely by *who* I am. Roy Cohn is not a homosexual. Roy Cohn is a heterosexual man . . . who fucks around with guys."

Gender, performativity and relationality

The first words spoken when a human being is born—these days even before birth—are: "It's a boy!" or "It's a girl!" This is, often enough, regardless of the biological information carried in genes or hormones that may subsequently give the speaker reason to doubt their original attribution of sex. This kind of speech is what the feminist philosopher, Judith Butler (1997), has called "performative speech"—it is not simply speech that names something, but speech that calls into being the thing it purports to be naming. It creates the "boy" or the "girl" at the moment of speaking. It is speech that ushers the new-born into a pre-existing order of what the child will be able to know, feel, or say about itself.

This notion of the performative can also be read, and *is* increasingly being read by relational psychoanalysts, as inevitably *relational*. The ways in which a child is likely to experience its psychic and physical self will be created and recreated in a relational matrix of speaking and touching, conscious and unconscious engagement, that repeats over and over again the performative: "You are a boy, you are a girl" until the child is able to perform the word "I", and take on responsibility for performing his or her own gender, by saying "*I* am a boy; *I* am a girl", in all the complex, often contradictory ways that we say these things to ourselves and others: by the ways we look (or can't look), dress (or can't dress), speak (or can't speak), feel (or can't feel), desire (or forbid ourselves from desiring). It is the culmination of this process that Freud identified as the Oedipus complex—the sexed, gendered, and sexually orientated entry into culture.

Freud's psychoanalytic discourse, notwithstanding his ambivalent oscillation between the biological and the constructed, was ultimately based on the axiom that: "Anatomy is destiny". That is, that biological reality dictates psychic reality. A post-modern view reverses the prescription: it is psychic reality that creates the body *as it is lived*. This has brought post-modernist views and relational approaches into close proximity with each other, since for relational psychoanalysis, psychic reality is by definition a *relational* reality.

We can begin to see a theory of performativity as potentially a relational theory. All performances, after all, require an audience. They are communications to an "other"—relational events—even, or perhaps particularly, when the other for whom we perform is internalized within us. The audience response will be likely to have a profound influence upon what performances feel possible or safe. Do we feel compelled to perform our genders in culturally prescribed ways to get a good review? As early as 1929, Joan Riviere, for instance, describes women using the strategy of feminine behaviour to camouflage their intellectual or practical competence from men.

> Womanliness therefore could be assumed and worn as a mask, both to hide [a woman's] . . . possession of masculinity and to avert the reprisals expected if she was found to possess it—much as a thief will turn out his pockets and ask to be searched to prove that he has not the stolen goods. The reader may now ask how I define womanliness or where I draw the line between genuine womanliness and the "masquerade". My suggestion is not, however, that there is any difference; whether radical or superficial, they are the same thing. [Riviere, 1929]

Post-modern gender theorists, and now relational psychoanalysts, have taken up and elaborated this understanding of "the masquerade", of gender as a fiction, albeit a fiction that is, paradoxically, passionately lived through the body (Goldner, 2003a). With each relational event we have opportunities to recreate ourselves. These recreations may be highly nuanced, complex, and various—so that we can have many-gendered selves varying according to the relational matrices in which we participate. But all these fictions will be written in and against the language and grammar of our binarily gendered cultural discourse.

Sexuality as a construction

This multi-layered complexity of gendered identity is beautifully illustrated in Kimberley Peirce's transgender odyssey *Boys Don't Cry* (Fox Searchlight, 1999). Lana and Brandon make love in the moonlight, during Lana's break from the night shift at her factory job. Brandon is different from the other men she knows—handsome, gentle. She feels she is in a trance making love with him. This romantic dream-like love-making scene between Lana and Brandon is intercut with her post-coital girly gossip session with her friends, Kate and Candace. The experience was so "intense", Lana tells them, that she "cannot talk about it". She tantalizes, they press for details. Finally, she admits, to their whoops of excitement, that she and Brandon "did it". But we, the audience, see what Kate and Candace cannot, and are aware of the discrepancies between the love scene action and Lana's subsequent account. We know that when Lana says: "And then we took off our clothes and went swimmin'", that she's elaborating, fabricating. She and Brandon didn't take off their clothes. Indeed, their lovemaking is predicated precisely upon the maintenance of the fantasy that Lana is a "woman"' and that Brandon is not, at least according to dominant gender discourse. Brandon isn't a "man", and Lana both knows it and chooses not to know it simultaneously.

But what do we, the viewers, think we have just seen? "Heterosexual" sex between a "man"' and a "woman"? "Lesbian" sex between two "women"? Or something else altogether? And how do we think the lovers in this scene experience themselves? Is Lana "really" a heterosexual woman? Or is she "really" a lesbian who can't face up to wanting another woman and who needs

Brandon to act male to make lesbianism acceptable? Is Brandon "really" a transsexual man, or "really" a lesbian who has to disguise her gender and sexuality in a violently homophobic social environment? Do we care, and if so, why? (For further discussion of these questions, see Butler, 2004.)

In contrast to the constructedness of gender, sexuality poses as authentic, nature in the raw, the animal in the human. The altered state of "otherness" we enter in sex seems to back this up. But we forget or repress that we have learned how to have sex, absorbed it from the culture, and the sexual tropes that seem most "natural" are, in fact, the tropes that simply conceal their constructedness under the guise of "biological" "bodily" urges, to which we just "give in". Once we denaturalize sex, though, we can begin to acknowledge its many manifestations as fantasies, created or co-created out of our culturally mediated psychic elaborations of relational experience. Far from being naturally "carried away" by sex, a certain machinery of fantasmatic backstage activity is required to stage any erotic performance. As Virginia Golder comments:

> The erotic . . . requires, like any piece of theatre, the suspension of disbelief. Turning up the houselights, even for a passing thought, breaks the spell. This is why we are afraid to analyse any sex that works, no matter how exalted or shameful. [Golder, 2003a, p. 123]

An essential part of that backstage machinery is the socially constructed phantasm of gender. Without it, we can't even imagine mounting a production. When we are "doing" sex, we are also simultaneously "doing" our gender, in a way that can enable the reinscription of that gender. For example, one of the spin-offs of heterosexual sex may be to reconfirm each partner in their gender performance, each partner believing in the reality of their own performance more implicitly, the more convincing, the more real the performance of the other. In the words of the immortal Aretha Franklin: "You make me feel like a natural woman".

In this scenario, the phantasm of heterosexuality can position itself as "authentic", while unreality and inauthenticity can be projected elsewhere. Homosexuals can then be seen as mere imitators of real (heterosexual) sex: after all, one of them must be the "boy", the other the "girl". Or transsexuals can be seen as imitators of "real" gender, authors of false bodies, genders, and sexualities. It's striking that at precisely the historical moment that homosexuality was finally being removed from the *Diagnostic and Statistical Manual*, gender identity disorder found its way in. Surgically and hormonally transsexed bodies currently carry the cultural burden of representing the ultimate dividing line between the binary categories of the "real" and the "false". Thus the picket fence between "them" and "us" has once again been shifted, but not removed.

In this vein, we could consider the "trans" nature of the differences between adult bodies and child bodies. There is shock and strangeness for the child in encountering the adult sexual body. There is alienness for the adult in the child's sexual body. Or the "transition" of puberty—we've all been there. Is the "trans" experience, therefore, less alien to us then we would like to think?

Judith Halberstam (1994, pp. 225–226) suggests that it is a ". . . cultural fiction that divides a sex from a transsex, a gender from a transgender". If all our sexes and genders are equally constructed, equally phantasmatic, then we could see the queer heterosexuality of Brandon and Lana in *Boys Don't Cry* as offering a deconstruction, not only of normative heterosexuality, but of sexuality itself. Brandon and Lana are not "mimicking" heterosexuality—they are holding up a mirror to show us how the stage machinery is worked for all of us.

Perhaps this could free us to wonder about other subtexts, more unexpected readings of more conventional sexual scripts. So what if Romeo, while consciously feeling himself to be a "real" man in bed with Juliet, is at the same time unconsciously identifying with Juliet's experience of making love as a "real" woman? What if Romeo's identification with Juliet even becomes conscious? What if Romeo wants to swap genders with Juliet altogether for the night until the house lights go up? What if Romeo wants to swap permanently?

How much psychoanalytic theorizing about sex has been in the service of warding off "gender panic" about such cross-identifications by projecting them on to homosexual subjectivities? How much lesbian and gay resistance to such theorizing has found itself defensively denying that such cross-identifications might take place? That they might even be an enjoyable part of a sexual repertoire for everyone, rather than a source of dread or a proof of inauthenticity? As David Schwartz (1995, p. 122) suggests: "Let us say that all human sexual practice is fetish, each one defending against wishes to transgress and falsely claiming that without *it* there can be no real arousal".

Some binary challenges (1): a perversion by any other name . . .

Psychoanalysis began with "perverse" sexualities—sexual practices with aims that Freud said arouse condemnation because they arouse disgust. Is "perversion" simply about the "yuck" factor, what we call a sexual activity that other people do that we would never see ourselves doing? How do we distinguish between perversion in this sense, and the use of sexuality—its deployment for the purposes of empowering one person at the expense of another?

Some relational practitioners are now asking whether it helps us and our clients to keep using this language of perversion, whether it tells us anything about a sexual fantasy or practice apart from the fact that we don't like it or approve of it. Does it simply preserve a dividing line between those practices and the ones we do approve of? Does it ensure that we, as therapists, remain the arbiters of where the line should be?

On the other hand, is there merit in retaining the notion of a perverse sexuality as a sexuality in which there is a failure of intersubjectivity? In which sexual subjects can only meet objects, objects that can be manipulated to achieve orgasm, but who can't be permitted any separate centre of sexual subjectivity of their own? This would have nothing to do with the polymorphousness of the activities, sexed bodies, or body parts involved, and nothing to do with the procreative intention or reproductive outcome of sex. It would have everything to do with the extent of intersubjectivity possible in the erotic encounter.

Some binary challenges (2): sexuality vs attachment

Binary thinking poses us with perhaps the most intractable of our Western sexual dilemmas: the paradoxical split between attachment and sexuality.

Do our clients have more difficulties with a taboo on attachment than a taboo on sex? Are clients unable to sustain sexual desire within lasting attachments? As Stephen Mitchell (2002) asked: "Can love last?" Is attachment felt to be a trap, a drag on our ability to explore our sexual selves? Zygmunt Bauman (2003) puts the dilemma of post-modern "liquid" lovers thus:

> Unbound, they must connect . . . None of the connections . . . are, however, guaranteed to last. Anyway, they need to be only loosely tied, so that they can be untied again, with little delay, when the settings change—as in liquid modernity they surely will, over and over again. (Bauman, 2003, p. vii.)

Does this binary of relationship versus freedom and risk map on to well-worn dichotomies between love and sex? Boredom and excitement; femininity and masculinity, attachment and sexuality? A post-modern sensibility will, of course, be sensitive to any hint of another Cartesian opposition being foisted upon us, and would consider the possibility that we are, in fact, simply grappling, yet again, with another manifestation of the fundamental binary of gender that divides us from each other. A post-modern approach would seek to explore ways of breaking down this either/or paradox, to enable us and our clients to think more fruitfully and creatively about the possibilities of both/and.

At the same time, such an approach would acknowledge the difficulties in resolving the conundrum of sex versus love as long as binary gender remains a fundamental discourse of power at the heart of our culture, one in which we are all caught up. It's a struggle to free ourselves from these deeply ingrained modes of experiencing. So, for example, Stephen Mitchell (2002) has suggested that secure attachment in adult relationships leads to a collusive deadness and predictability between couples. They can no longer risk the intensity of sexual passion, lest it rock the boat and destabilize the relationship's safety. For Mitchell, attachment and intimacy make sex scarier, because of the risk of loss, keeping the binary intact. But we don't have to see it this way. Virginia Goldner (2003b), by contrast, responds that it is precisely secure attachment and intimacy that creates the safety to free us to explore with each other sexually. And Jessica Benjamin (2003) questions why we need to see sexual thrills as the Other to ordinary love. Why, she asks, can't we have a sexual theory that can encompass both the thrill of deep intimacy that is transformative of each other's self-states, and the thrill of the dissociative and intrapsychic, without needing to decide that one of these possibilities is healthy and the other is not? Sexual passion demands a capacity to hold the tension between intersubjective intimacy and the intrapsychic fantasy that fuels lust.

As Jessica Benjamin (2003) puts it: "That tendency to draw a hard line between vanilla and Cherry Garcia is surely tied . . . to some of our other 'favorite flavors' in splitting: attachment from eros, light from darkness, maternal from sexual".

Some binary challenges (3): "Babies and their mothers"—the sexual chicken and the autoerotic egg: where does the sexuality come from?

Attachment theory has been criticized for focusing on external observation of the interactions in the mother–baby relationship, to the exclusion of issues of sexuality that remain at the heart of post-Freudian psychoanalysis. How can infant observation tell us anything about what's happening in the mother's or baby's fantasy world, in the sexual unconscious? What has happened, we are asked, to sexual fantasy, to infantile sexuality, to Oedipus? Where has Eros gone in attachment theory? Are attachment theorists returning to a pre-Freudian innocence, where there *is* no sexuality—not in the baby and not in the mother? And if we're not saying this, then how *do* we say the sexuality gets into the baby, without reverting to innate pre-cultural sexual drives that just appear all by themselves, outside of any relational context?

We are only beginning to think about this, as we've been so busy establishing the impact of relationality on the more general formation of subjectivity. French theorists, however, in particular Jean Laplanche (1976), have long been retheorizing infantile sexuality, and its relationship to the sexuality of adult carers. Now it seems that attachment theory and French psychoanalytic theory are undergoing a rapprochement, where the eroticism of the mother–baby dyad can become a joint topic of exploration.

Laplanche (1976) returns to Freud's abandoned seduction theory and rehabilitates it as a general theory of the genesis of sexuality and sexual fantasy. Sexuality—the parent's—infuses the relational matrix in which attachment takes place and, in the handling and care that the baby receives, the mother's own eroticism is consciously or unconsciously aroused.

Presumably, how the eroticism of nursing, or of any other aspect of caring for her baby, is experienced by any particular mother, and communicated to her baby, will depend upon how comfortable that individual mother is with her own sexual feelings, and whether she is able to manage the erotic elements of the relationship without horror or shame or the acting out of abuse. In other words, how well she is able to negotiate the binary.

We are left with questions—does the infant's sexuality only arise as a response to the sexuality of the adult? Or is there a spontaneous autoerotism with its own genesis? Is the enigmatic sexual message coming from the other's unconscious always traumatic, as Laplanche assumes, or is the autoerotism it sparks playfully pleasurable in its own right? (Widlocher, 2001. pp. 19–22). Do the autoerotic fantasies the child creates constitute the "missing link" between the object world—the world of external relationships, the attachment world—and the intrapsychic world of pleasure? Is object seeking thus converted into pleasure seeking? And how does the infant's fantasy experience then feed back into the attachment relationships themselves? As Peter Fonagy has put it:

> Since the vehicle of infantile sexuality is the experience of the object world, it is inevitable that subtle, bi-directional causal relationships are rapidly established and external experience now reinterpreted as autoerotic activity comes to profoundly alter the child's actual interaction. [Fonagy, 2001, p. 59]

What happens when this subtle oscillation between reality and fantasy is disrupted? When the liminal and transitional either becomes too real and thus terrifying (as in sexual abuse) or utterly fantastical and thus disconnected entirely from the object world? What are the consequences for adult sexuality and what are the implications for the psychotherapeutic relationship?

Conclusion: "liquid love, liquid selves"

In 1915 Freud described the difficulty of the struggle for change within a psychoanalysis—how a "psychical inertia", that opposes change and fights against progress and recovery, is a fundamental precondition of a neurotic symptom (Freud, 1915f).

In post-modern parlance, I think that we are becoming accustomed to referring to this phenomenon not as fixation, as Freud named it, but as reification—the solidifying of an identity or a relational paradigm into a "thing", rigid, unchangeable, universally expectable in all circumstances. Freud located its causes in very early linkages between feelings and objects—the relational matrix itself, within the erotic crucible of which, as Laplanche (1976) has pointed out, the creation of both an ego and an unconscious are made possible.

The heat of that early erotic passion is what originally provides the energy for the forging of a self, and we need the heat generated by adult erotic passion to reforge what has previously been wrought in early relational experience. Perhaps it's no accident that Eros, the combining or uniting principle who first appears in Greek myth as emerging from Chaos at the beginning of the world, reappears as either a winged baby or an adolescent boy. We might see these mythological figures as representing the points in the life cycle at which Western culture has attributed to the erotic its most potent shot at stoking up the fires of self re-creation. Of course, psychoanalysis had not been invented then. We might consider whether Freud's potent discoveries—the erotic transference, and its contemporary intersubjective partner, the erotic counter-transference—take their power from the potential to provide another chance for solidly reified, yet painful, self states to reheat, liquefy once more and change their form.

Attachment-based and relational therapists are now asking themselves whether the concept of so-called security of attachment as a therapeutic goal means that we are also seeking to "secure" our identities, or whether too rigid a sense of self is the cause of much human misery. Jessica Benjamin (2003) suggests that: "Attachment . . . should ideally create a container for the constant change and impermanence of human life . . . ."

Judith Butler has spoken recently of the importance of philosophy in enabling us to think about change in our sexual and gender possibilities:

> ... politically it is important that people ask the question 'what is possible?' and believe in possibility. Because without the notion of possibility there is no motion forward. The idea that people might live their gender in a different way, or they might live their sexuality in a different way, that there might be room for a liveable, sustainable, pleasurable, happy, politically informed life out of the closet. Philosophy makes people think about possible roles, it gives people the chance to think the world as if it was otherwise. And people need that. [Butler, 2001]

Let us hope that what she says here about the promise of philosophy can now, at last, begin to be said of a queer and relational psychoanalysis.

References

Bauman, Z. (2003). *Liquid Love: On the Frailty of Human Bonds.* Cambridge: Polity Press

Benjamin, J. (2003). What happens when love lasts? An exploration of intimacy and erotic life. International Association for Relational Psychoanalysis and Psychotherapy, Online Colloquium, March 2003 at http://www.iarpp.org

Berger, J. (1972). *Ways of Seeing.* SOS Free Stock [reprinted Harmondsworth: Penguin Books, 1990].

Bienen, A., & Peirce, K. (1999). *Boys Don't Cry.* Fox Searchlight.

Butler, J. (1997). *Excitable Speech: A Politics of the Performative.* New York: Routledge

Butler, J. (2001). The desire for philosophy: Interview with Judith Butler, the American philosopher, during her visit to in Berlin, in May 2001, invited by the American Academy. The interview was conducted by Regina Michalik (LOLA press). http://www.lola-press.org/elec2/artenglish/butl_e.htm

Butler, J. (2004). Changing the subject: Judith Butler's politics of radical resignification. In: S. Salih & J. Butler (Eds.), *The Judith Butler Reader* (pp. 325–356). Oxford: Blackwell Publishing.

Dean, T. (2003). Lacan and queer theory. In: Jean-Michel Rabate (Ed.), *The Cambridge Companion to Lacan* (pp. 238–252). Cambridge: Cambridge University Press, 2003.

Fairfield, S., Layton, L., & Stack, C. (Eds.) (2002). *Bringing the Plague: Toward a Postmodern Psychoanalysis.* New York: Other Press.

Fonagy, P. (2001). Infantile sexuality as a creative process. In: D. Widlocher (Ed.), *Infantile Sexuality and Attachment* (pp. 55–63). New York: Other Press.

Foucault, M. (1978). *The History of Sexuality. Vol. I: An Introduction.* R. Hurley (Trans.). New York: Pantheon.

Freud, S. (1905d). Three essays on the theory of sexuality. *S.E., 7:* 125. London: Hogarth.

Freud, S. (1915f). A case of paranoia running counter to the psycho analytic theory of the disease. *S.E., 14:* 263. London: Hogarth.

Freud, S. (1925j). Some psychical consequences of the anatomical distinction between the sexes. *S.E., 19:* 243. London: Hogarth.

Freud, S. (1937c). Analysis terminable and interminable *S.E., 23:* 211. London: Hogarth.

Gauntlett, D. (1998). Judith Butler. www.theory.org.uk/ctr-butl.htm

Goldner, V. (2003a). Ironic gender/authentic sex. *Studies in Gender and Sexuality, 4:* 113–139.

Goldner, V. (2003b). Attachment and eros: opposed or enthralled? In "What happens when love lasts? An exploration of intimacy and erotic life. International Association for Relational Psychoanalysis and Psychotherapy, Online Colloquium, March 2003 at http://www.iarpp.org

Halberstam, J. (1994). Quoted in Katrina Roen: Transgender theory and embodiment: the risk of racial marginalisation. *Journal of Gender Studies, 10*(3): 2001.

Kuhn, T. (1962). *The Structure of Scientific Revolutions.* Chicago: University of Chicago Press.

Kushner, T. (1992). *Angels in America: A Gay Fantasia on National Themes: Millennium Approaches Part 1.* London: Nick Hern Books.

Lacan, J. (1966). The mirror stage as formative of the function of the I as revealed in psychoanalytic experience. In: Lacan: *Ecrits: a selection* (pp. 1–8). A. Sheridan (Trans.). London: Routledge.

Laplanche, J. (1976)[1985]. *Life and Death in Psychoanalysis.* Baltimore, MD: The Johns Hopkins University Press.

Layton, L. (1998). *Who's That Girl? Who's That Boy? Clinical Practice Meets Postmodern Gender Theory.* Northvale, NJ: Jason Aronson.

May, R. (1995). Re-reading Freud on homosexuality. In: T. Domenici & R. Lesser (Eds.), *Disorienting Sexuality: Psychoanalytic Reappraisals of Sexual Identities* (pp. 153–165). London: Routledge.

Mitchell, S. A. (2002). *Can Love Last? The Fate of Romance over Time*. New York: W. W. Norton.

Nichols, M. (2003). *Angels in America*. HBO Films.

Riviere, J. (1929). Womanliness as masquerade. In: V. Burgin, J. Donald & C. Caplan (Eds.), *Formations of Fantasy* (pp. 35–44). London: Methuen, 1986.

Schwartz, D. (1995). Current Psychoanalytic Discourses on Sexuality. In: T. Domenici & R. Lesser (Eds.), *Disorienting Sexuality: Psychoanalytic Reappraisals of Sexual Identities* (pp. 115–126). London: Routledge, 1995.

Wachowski, D., & Wachowski, L. (co-directors) (1999). *The Matrix*. Warner Bros.

Widlocher, D. (2001). Primary love and infantile sexuality. In: D. Widlocher (Ed.), *Infantile Sexuality and Attachment* (pp. 1–35). New York: Other Press.

Zizek, S. (1999). The Matrix, or two sides of perversion. *Philosophy Today, 43*.

Clinical implications of queer theory

A response to Judy Yellin's paper

Joanna Ryan

J udy's paper is a *tour de force*, mapping a very complex, dense, and changing territory in a delightful and engaging way.

I would like to elaborate on some of Judy's arguments as to why any psychoanalysis, any psychotherapy, attachment-based or otherwise, should take note of and incorporate queer theory approaches. I want to address the question of how we relate what Judy has so clearly laid out to clinical practice. I hope that in the ensuing discussion many people will raise their own experiences of how this kind of approach has been helpful to them, or indeed express their doubts about it.

For myself, in writing *Wild Desires and Mistaken Identities* (O'Connor & Ryan, 1993), queer theory ideas were essential in trying to understand how psychoanalysis, which originally had so much liberal and inclusive potential, could also lend itself to so much excluding thought and practice. Queer theory, as part of post-modernism, has also been helpful in evolving new clinical understandings in working with lesbians and gay men in therapy. Here I want to raise a series of issues that often arise in clinical work.

Queer theory in itself does not purport to be a theory that either arises from, or relates to, clinical practice. However, it does relate to how experience, identity, subjectivity and desire are lived and constructed within language and the social order. Queer theory is in this way experience—near, and therefore very relevant to the phenomena of the consulting room. It is also quite abstract in its concern with presuppositions and conceptual schema, and there-fore relevant to how therapists think about what they hear, indeed to how they hear and respond.

First, in analysing the power of the dominant discourse, we are forced to consider the ways in which, whatever our oppositional or alternative stances, we are also constituted as subjects within discourses that we did not choose. As Judith Butler (1997) argues in *The Psychic Life of Power*, as well as thinking of power as something that presses on the subject from outside, that subordinates and produces opposition and resistance, we also need to see how power forms subjects: how it is what we depend on for our existence, and what partly constitutes us as the beings we are. There can be no true self or pristine notion of the subject outside power.

In psychoanalytic terms, this notion of the interiority of the operation of power is not unintelligible. Indeed, in the notion of "identification with the aggressor" we can find a mechanism that allows us to put clinical flesh on the bones of queer theory. We can also locate it in the common clinical experience we have of those who unavoidably form passionate attachments that are enactments of previous dependent relationships with hostile, rejecting, exploit-ative, but also exciting and powerful figures. The desire for and fusion with the hated object—a fusion that can be so elusive and so hard to separate from, whatever the amount of protest or indigna-tion, or sense of victimhood—is another indication of the way that the very existence and persistence of oneself can seem to depend upon re-enacting the unacceptable conditions of subordination. Or, as Judy puts it in her paper, we are continually negotiating the tension between resistance and compliance. One quite creative way of moving beyond this tension is the playful, but none the less serious appropriation of the norm: as in drag, as in "We're queer, we're here, get used to it" and indeed, as in gay marriage, all of which are different kinds of appropriations. The high political profile that gay and lesbian marriage has in the USA, the threat it is supposed to be to heterosexual marriage, is testimony to how vital questions of power are involved in any consideration of sexuality.

The concreteness with which issues of sexual orientation are often posed is another arena in which an understanding of the discursive status of gender binaries can help us avoid mirroring this very concreteness, and the sense of the given exclusivity of the either/or. In what follows I give a clinical example of the usefulness of this understanding, written up at greater length in Ryan (1997). All possibly identifying details are changed in this and all following clinical vignettes.

> A patient, who persistently and repetitively said through many years of therapy that she couldn't decide whether she was lesbian or heterosexual, exerted enormous pressure on the therapist to help her decide. Detailed exploration of the specifics of each orientation for her, in terms of the kinds of desires, anxieties, experiences, did not yield any movement in the direction of the certainty she ostensibly wanted, or towards any satisfying relationship. Rather, any sustained attention within sessions to one sexual orientation would almost always lead her to assert the possibility of the other orientation. Her actual relationships—mainly with women, but sometimes with men—were rendered deeply unsatisfying by overwhelming feelings of the other as no good or else of herself as always rejected. There were many defensive sources of this persistent oscillation between genders and sexualities, and of the demand for certainty. This certainty was kept wholly hypothetical, and gradually it was possible to explore the underlying terrors that attached to any intimate relationship with anyone of whatever gender, wherein she felt either completely obliterated or else had to obliterate the other.

> The pressure the therapist felt to help this patient "decide" between men and women as sexual objects was a counter-transference mirroring of the patient's seemingly unanswerable dilemma. In other words, the phantasmatic and symptomatic nature of the patient's dilemma was in danger of being replaced, for the therapist as for the patient, by an insistence or belief that there was a real either/or choice to be made, and one that would have a definitional status as to who the patient was. An awareness of the discursive nature and constitutive power of gender binaries enabled the therapist to help the patient to give up the quest for a "decision" and see her dilemmas in a less concrete and constraining way.

What such issues concerning sexual orientation may also raise is the very status of bisexuality within our thinking. Bisexuality has done a lot of liberal work within psychoanalysis, and it is no accident that the most homophobic period within our discipline was inaugurated by the abandonment of Freud's assumption of universal bisexuality in the middle of the last century. However, what do we think now? My impression is that not many of us think in bisexual terms about our patients, especially those who present as heterosexual. Some gay theorists have, from a gay specific position, wanted to opt for a notion of exclusive and constitutional homosexuality, others have argued for seeing all sexuality as a bisexual continuum. Is the queer theory assumption of the fluidity of sexuality the same as the Freudian one of universal bisexuality? There is an argument to be made that the psychoanalytic concept of bisexuality, useful as it has been, really consists in the postulated coexistence within one person of two heterosexual desires, tied as it is to notions of masculinity and femininity (Butler, 1990). In other words, it reinstates heterosexuality just as it appears to open this up. Furthermore, within the psychoanalytic canon, bisexuality is only an original or infantile state, never an adult one, other than in the unconscious, always something to be resolved.

In clinical practice we are often confronted by people whose adult life experiences are bisexual but who do not describe themselves in this way. This is partly to do with the problematics of identity. Bisexual identities are not, as the bisexual literature attests, that easily assumed, or lived out, or even recognized. I think the field is wide open for much greater clinical exploration of different bisexualities, and also of the play of the inter-relationships between homo- and heterosexual desires. A queer theory approach would see in this interplay desires and passions that may be vehicles for each other, or embedded within each other, and with multiple identificatory positions. This is different from the position of seeing bisexuality as an oscillation between different desires and different objects, where the supposition of oscillation inevitably pathologizes bisexuality as inconsistent, infantile, or unstable. We may find with one person that they express very similar conflicts and needs in their sexual relationships with both men and women; for another that very distinct desires are in play with sexual partners of different genders. And this only concerns actual gender and not felt,

fantasized or experienced aspects of gender, in which the combina-
tion of differently gendered aspects in one person is what is felt to
be attractive, or not.

An important issue where queer theory approaches are differentiated from other approaches is the status of developmental theory,
and attempts to construct gay or lesbian psychologies. Kenneth
Lewe (1988), in his ground-breaking book *The Psychoanalytic Theory
of Male Homosexuality*, traces various different routes to adult homosexuality within the Freudian canon of the Oedipus complex. His
detailed pluralizing of the many possible histories that gay men
may present with can be extremely helpful. Historically, however,
the almost exclusive focus on the "why" of sexual orientation has
been extremely problematic. It has led to the neglect of the lived
experiences of growing up gay or lesbian, the strengths that are
needed for this as well as the painfulness. Isay (1993) takes a different developmental stance: within his framework of seeing gay
sexuality as having constitutional origins (which is itself debatable)
he looks at the "how" of development. One especially helpful
insight has been his focus on gay boys' relationships with their
fathers, and how the rejection and hostility that some men report
can be seen as formed by the unconscious distancing on the part of
the father as a reaction to the boy's not yet acknowledged sexuality.

Critiques of developmental theory are also alive in the more
recent argument by two authors, Auchinloss and Vaughan (2001),
in a relatively mainstream journal. They criticize the notion that
what is needed is a new psychoanalytic theory of homosexuality,
and argue that such a demand is a request for more information
about the supposed object of scrutiny, rather than a reflection on
what therapists are doing or thinking in relation to homosexuality.
Their somewhat timid conclusion, that more or better listening is
required, although welcome in itself, does not address what
prevents therapists from doing so, that is, it does not address the
powerful countertransferential responses that surround this
subject, influenced by the complex mix of personal anxieties,
cultural forces and conceptual biases.

To the extent that people with various non-normative sexualities
might be said to have something in common with each other, then
I would argue that this can best be understood in terms of the
far-reaching effects of how the whole apparatus of thought and

practice around sexuality constructs our identities, our felt options, the forms our desires take, and also how it gets written on our bodies. It can also be understood from the perspective of the necessity for survival, for finding a viable sense of self and adequate self-esteem, of finding something in common, that is, breaking down the isolation that can be such a common feature of adolescent gay and lesbian experience, and in doing so forging common identities or lifestyles. It is here that a psychoanalytic understanding of homophobia in its diverse manifestations is essential, and yet this has scarcely begun.

The shift for a therapist towards thinking in queer theory terms, rather than only developmentally, is to open up many questions and ways of seeing experiences that did not exist before. Judy provides many examples of this enlarging effect. For example, the very commonly expressed fear that gay or lesbian desires betoken a defect of masculinity or femininity as in "Am I a proper man if I love this man or allow myself as a man to be desired by a man?", is often taken to mean that homosexuality really is an expression of gender identity disorder, something that is still widely taught. From a different, queer perspective it illustrates the inevitable entwining within our hegemonic discourses of issues of sexual and gender identity, the understanding that in doing sex we are simultaneously doing gender. *Wild Desires and Mistaken Identities* provided clinical examples of the many and varied connections and disconnections of sexuality and gender that can be experienced (O'Connor & Ryan, 1993).

In these areas language can be crucial: do you find yourself describing a lesbian with a butch presentation as masculine and why? Does she? If she herself uses the language of maleness how do you understand that? The perspective that masculinity, whatever it may be taken to be, is not the necessary property of men, that female masculinity is itself and not just a poor imitation of male masculinity, can help a patient develop a less self-hating and more dynamic and playful attitude to those aspects of herself she sees in that way, as the following vignette illustrates.

A patient, who with a great deal of conflict saw herself as a lesbian, referred frequently to a persecutory sense that no one saw her as a woman, and indeed that other women were only attracted to her in as much as she offered herself as essentially male. She hated this sense of what she called her maleness, because it made her feel such an inadequate woman, but at the same time experienced it as a source of having something desirable sexually. Unconsciously she had identified herself as a sexual being with a male paternal figure, in her case a very problematic one, and it was helpful for the therapist to realize that it was these problematic features of the paternal identification, not the maleness *per se*, that was the difficulty. The patient was enabled to arrive at a much less troubling sense of her maleness, to take pleasure in these aspects of herself that were indeed attractive to other women, and to cease experiencing what had felt like an intrusive and compulsive masculinity as blotting out her sense of herself as a woman; rather, it became a more creative part of herself.

Such an approach can also help us think about gender issues in relation to same-sex parenting, and the conflicts that lesbian or gay parents may find themselves faced with.

Another area in which queer theory is very relevant is in relation to casual or anonymous gay male sex. Many therapists find it difficult to work without resort to the generalized formulations of this being a defence against intimacy, part-object relating, or an extreme form of splitting. While such formulations certainly can have their place, they can also be defensive, hostile, or anxious reactions on the part of the therapist.

A man who came to therapy because of depression and a chaotic underachieving lifestyle that left him depleted, would start almost every session with descriptions of the sex that he had had with men whom he had transiently met in saunas. The descriptions tended to be full of the physical details but with very little fantasy content that could be articulated. The therapist found herself not wanting to hear about the sexual details, feeling disturbed and overwhelmed by the anonymity and transitoriness of what was described. She tried to get the patient to provide more emotional content. This was felt by the patient as a condemnation of his activities, an attempt to deprive him of his pleasures, and for a time the therapy became stalemated. It was only with a great deal of effort on the therapist's part, in examining the source of her own very difficult feelings, combined with extensive reading in the gay and queer literature, that she was enabled to find a more facilitative perspective.

This is an illustration of Judy's point that sources of thought from outside the psychoanalytic field are essential. The lessening of the therapist's counter-transference reactions that such a perspective enabled, in turn led to a much more productive exploration both of the pleasures and disappointments of the casual sex and also, in this case, of the patient's conflicts with more intimate relationships. It also helped them to address the questions of how risky or compulsive the behaviour was, and the issue of safe sex.

The historical, legal, and cultural legacy of gay sexuality was a vital framework here. So also was the recognition that anonymous or casual sex can be an important phenomenon in its own right, with its own specific pleasures, both physical and psychological, that need to be acknowledged and explored. I would argue for a notion that sex can be pursued simply as sex, and that this does not necessarily betoken an inability to relate erotically in other ways at other times, with a known partner or within an intimate relationship. Many people are capable of both, and at various times in their lives. Object-relations theory, in its departure from Freudian metapsychology, has tended to reduce sex to love or attachment, hence the difficulty this conference is attempting to address.

Finally, many countertransferential issues may arise in working with erotic same-gender transferences. There are a vast array of phenomena here, with many sources. One example pertains to a presumptively heterosexual female therapist who finds it difficult to take up and explore sexual issues with a lesbian patient, who becomes inhibited, does not know what to say, and finds herself inwardly freezing at transferential erotic material. Her ability to make therapeutically helpful imaginative identifications deserts her. Knowing about another woman's erotic desires for her may press uncomfortably upon the whole way she has constructed herself as a heterosexual subject, however open and liberal minded she may be. In one version (Butler, 1997) of the constitution of the heterosexual subject, it is not just repression but radical foreclosure of any erotic homosexual love that is involved, a rigorous barring of such desire, in which the loss involved cannot be recognized and therefore cannot be mourned. It is this unacknowledged loss that is foundational to a certain heterosexual version of the subject. From a psychoanalytic perspective it is not hard to see the various unconscious and pathological consequences, including distancing, hostility, and envy, that can arise from such unacknowledged love and loss, where someone's very identity depends on this foreclosure. The conscious attempts of well-intentioned therapists may not, without some further understanding, be enough to prevent the kinds of reactions described in this example. The kind of approach Judy has outlined can help overcome the various difficulties we, as therapists, may encounter in talking with our patients about sex and eroticism, and in sometimes becoming the object within the transference of such desires.

References

Auchinloss, E., & Vaughan, S. (2001). Psychoanalysis and homosexuality: do we need a new theory? *Journal of American Psychoanalytic Association*, *49*: 1157–1186.

Butler, J. (1990). *Gender Trouble: Feminism and the Subversion of Identity*. London: Routledge.

Butler, J. (1997). *The Psychic Life of Power: Theories in Subjection*. Palo Alto, CA: Stanford University Press.

Isay, R. (1993). *Being Homosexual: Gay Men and their Development*. Harmondsworth: Penguin.

Lewe, K. (1988). *The Psychoanalytic Theory of Male Homosexuality*. London: Quartet.

O'Connor, N., & Ryan, J. (1993). *Wild Desires and Mistaken Identities: Lesbianism and Psychoanalysis*. London: Virago [reprinted London: Karnac, 2003].

Ryan, J. (1997). Fantasies and problematics of identity. In: M. Lawrence & M. Maguire (Eds.), *Psychotherapy with Women: Feminist Perspectives* (pp. 95–104). London: Macmillan.

Attachment and sexuality

What does our clinical experience tell us?

Joseph Schwartz

Introduction

D ue to the culturally loaded nature of sexuality, it is particularly important to emphasize that case material is sensitive, especially so when countertransferential feelings are involved. As such one must be careful to view clinical material from the clinician's experience of the therapeutic encounter, avoiding the temptation to "get in on the case". With this method in hand, I will discuss how, in a clinical exploration with colleagues, we found ourselves concluding that, in the first approximation, sexual feelings are like any other feelings in the therapeutic relationship, to be explored with openness and interest without foreclosure. I will discuss some of the special difficulties that can occur in working clinically with sexuality in the consulting room and some theoretical implications, particularly for male sexuality.

There is, of course, no such thing as simple clinical observation. We always approach our clients with theory in mind. It would be impossible to be an effective clinician without a framework for understanding and relating to our clients. So the question of what our clinical experience tells us about sexuality is far from a trivial project. We have to be careful not simply to hear what we already know.

Yet, at the same time, clinical experience is what we base all of our theory on. It is our primary data, so to speak. So, in the extremely sensitive and historically loaded question of sexuality we are on difficult ground. On the one hand we must learn from our clients. On the other we can't learn without a prior framework.

I describe here some of the processes I and colleagues at the Centre of Attachment-based Psychoanalytic Psychotherapy engaged in a project of exploring our clinical work to see how we handled issues around sexuality and to see what we could learn from our clinical experience (Laschinger, Purnell, Schwartz, White, & Wingfield, 2004).

Method

Because of the sensitive nature of sexuality, we realized very early on that in order to discuss issues of sexuality, particularly erotic counter-transference, we had to focus on the clinician's experience and avoid temptations to get in on the case, so to speak, with alternative interpretations or judgemental questions along the lines of "Why did you do that?"

We assumed, as given, that we all shared a common clinical perspective as attachment-based psychoanalytic psychotherapists. We had been frequently asked by colleagues within other orientations and by our own trainees how one works with sexuality in an attachment-based approach to clinical work. We found we had no simple summary to present and we formed a study group to see how each of us worked with these issues. We assumed we were dealing with sexuality in an attachment-based way because that is the way we all approach our work. The question was, how to describe it?

We found in the first approximation that sexual feelings appeared naturally in our clinical work more or less like any other feelings and that they were not the *sine qua non* of our work, as they might be in more classically based approaches. Although sexuality was frequently the focus of much of our therapeutic work we found that in our practices eating problems, for example, were far more prevalent as presenting difficulties.

Theoretical stances

Bowlby had sharply distinguished the attachment system from the reproductive (sexual) system. We disagreed with Bowlby and much attachment research theorizing. In our clinical work this dichotomy simply did not apply: sexuality, love, and safety were inextricably entwined. Based on our clinical experience, at the level of human emotional life, it did not seem possible to distinguish between these two hypothesized biological systems.

We also rejected the traditional pairing of sexuality and aggression coming originally from Freud's theoretical approach of there being two basic human drives—reproduction (sexuality) and self-preservation (aggression), (Kernberg, 1991; Stoller, 1979). Instead we were in agreement with the relational approach of Stephen Mitchell (1988), of a human sexuality without aggression and, indeed, a human sexuality without drive theory at all.

Bowlby's (1985) writing on anger and aggression situated these feelings in the context of a person's emotional response to experiences of loss or separation, a rupture in their attachment relationships. We believe that the mistaken intertwining of sexuality and aggression has occurred precisely because of an underdeveloped understanding of the relationship between sexuality and attachment. Feelings of sexual desire provide an essential link between internal and external: a passport to the outside world and part of the adult need for attachment. Within an attachment framework we can then speak of a sexuality of hope with an associated attachment dynamic affirming our right to our subjectivity. And we can have similarly a sexuality of despair, the sexuality of one whose subjectivity has been denied by past and present attachment failure, a sadomasochistic sexuality that denies the other their subjectivity.

Some clinical observations of sexuality in relation to early attachment histories

In histories characterized by early sexual intrusion we found the frequent occurrence of intrusive fantasies and aggressive sadomasochistic repetitions.

In histories characterized by unrepaired losses we found adults suffering loneliness and isolation, anxious/insecure attachments where conflicted longings for closeness can lead to needs for bodily affect regulation, such as masturbation, to calm and soothe.

In histories with a series of disruptive separations a pattern of anger and aggression may infuse sexual relationships.

Four themes emerging from our collective clinical exploration

1. Sexual fantasies can be worked with by free association in the same way we work with dreams. Exploration of a fantasy of being penetrated by a woman with a penis uncovered past experience of humiliation at the hands of a mother in a pattern of disorganized attachment where a needed attachment figure is also a threatening one. In addition, the fantasy also represents a need to control a woman by having something she wants (sex).

2. Strikingly, early abandonment and/or unresolved losses lead to what one of us (BL) characterized as a melancholy sexuality. Instead of a torrid jungle of untamed id drives, the client suffers an arctic wasteland, cold and devoid of relationships.

3. In all attachment difficulties there can be a profound insecurity about inhabiting one's body, with all the implications this might have for a person's capacity for engaging in intimate sexual relationships.

4. In cases where strong erotic feelings are present in the consulting room, it is essential to be able to enjoy erotic feelings in the counter-transference without conflict or need. We also noted for future work the important paper by Davies (1998) questioning whether there is room for normal, non-countertransferential, adult sexual feelings in the therapy relationship.

What does our clinical experience tell us about male psychology and sexuality?

Fairbairn's clinical experience told him, at times quite forcefully in the voice of his patient, that the human being was not pleasure seeking but was object seeking: "You keep telling me I want this and that instinct satisfied when what I really want is a father" (Fairbairn, 1946). For a number of reasons, including his interest in science, his isolation in Scotland, and his lack of interest in the turmoil of the British Psychoanalytic Society of the 1940s, Fairbairn felt free enough to develop his understanding of object relations into the first British relational psychoanalysis. Fairbairn was to the inner world what Bowlby was to the outer world.

With both Fairbairn and Bowlby emphasizing, in what is now undoubtedly the case, that the human being has a primary drive towards relationship–attachment, a first question would be where does Freud's pleasure seeking fit in? And here Fairbairn followed scientific discipline in a model fashion. Instead of simply dismissing pleasure seeking, Fairbairn included it in his framework. He asked himself: how can I understand pleasure seeking within an object relations framework? His answer was: pleasure seeking is a deterioration of object relationships.

If we accept the framework that the human being is fundamentally relationship seeking, we then have an interesting way to understand certain aspects of male sexuality and psychology as it has developed in the West. Dinnerstein (1976) analysed the dynamical consequences of absent fathers in the child-rearing practices of the Western nuclear families of the last 100 years, practices characterized by absent productive fathers and home-based reproductive mothers. Girl children can then have a merged relationship with their parent of the same sex (itself leading to dynamical problems). But boy children are forced to engage in a defensive separation from their opposite sexed parent. Recall the jibes of "mama's boy" visited on any boy child who sought to retain a connection with his mother around the age of seven or eight.

Boys are pressured/forced to move into a relational vacuum leading to a tendency towards avoidant attachment, making for a tendency towards relationless sexuality in adult life. Men tend to be pleasure seeking in their sexual relationships as a consequence of the deterioration of object relationships in their boyhood.

There is more. Fairbairn recognized that our fundamental relational needs extend into adulthood. Instead of a model of adult *in*dependence, he outlined a three-stage model of human psychological needs in which we move from a stage of infantile dependence through a long transitional stage of childhood to a final stage of mature dependence. Women, almost without exception, will have noticed that men have a particular difficulty with the stage of mature dependence. This difficulty has been effectively hidden by the myth of male independence, as has been analysed by Eichenbaum and Orbach (1983), who have observed that male adult dependency needs are met by women not only without being acknowledged, but without being acknowledged that adult men have dependency needs in the first place.

Clinical vignettes supporting this description of a male psychology characterized by avoidant attachment and pleasure seeking in place of object relating will be well known to any clinician who works with men.

What does our clinical experience tell us about how we get a sexual body?

Based on extensive clinical experience of working with troubled bodies, Orbach (1999, 2004) created a framework for understanding the developmental dynamics of corporeality. Following Winnicott's idea of a false self, Orbach has introduced the idea of the false body as an unstable, labile body not quite inhabited by its owner. The body we actually inhabit is a socially created body. Boy babies are handled very differently from girl babies and any bodily insecurity the mother has is communicated to the infant in the course of its development. We acquire our bodies in relationship with our caregivers. In particular, parental feelings about their own sexuality will be transmitted along with everything else.

Davies (1998) has a particularly vivid example of how our attitudes towards sexuality can affect our children's sexual development. She describes a girl saying to her mother: "Mummy, it happies me when I touch myself there. You touch me there."

We understand from Davies that the mother in question told her daughter that touching herself was fine but it was the kind of thing she did for herself. As Davies points out, this relationship to childhood sexual pleasure is very different from the way parents relate to other feelings. In cases of anger, upset, jealousy, envy, the parent will sit with a child explaining, helping to metabolize and effectively socialize these feelings. Not so with childhood sexual feelings. We instruct our children to make this exploration on their own. We have yet to understand the full clinical consequences of our culture's awkward silence on matters of childhood sexuality. But it is clearly something worth thinking carefully about. And this awkwardness can extend to our consulting rooms. Sweetnam (1999) is among the very few clinicians who have written about exploring in close detail the quality of her client's sexual experiences. We have a way to go.

Conclusion

I'd like to make two concluding points on how we can learn about sexuality and attachment from our clinical practice. The first is about therapeutic neutrality. Over the past fifty years therapeutic neutrality has all too frequently been taken to mean that the therapist shows no reaction to what he or she is hearing, a version of the blank screen model of the therapeutic relationship. But therapeutic neutrality in Freud's hands always meant openness, a lack of prejudgment to what a patient may say to us (Orbach, 1999). "Listening with the third ear" (Reik, 1948), requires that we try to hear with interest and openness what our clients tell us about their sexual experience. This can be difficult.

Second, I want to offer a vignette from the natural sciences that may be useful as we attempt to learn from our clinical experience. We tend to be reticent about offering up the understandings we generate for ourselves in our clinical work, leaving it to unspecified others or the historical greats to speak to our experience. This reticence cannot get us very far.

Wolfgang Pauli Jr was known as the conscience of physics during the quantum revolution (paradigm shift) of 1920s physics. A *wunderkind*, he was known for his unrelentingly accurate critiques of his colleagues work. He concluded one highly critical book review with the comment: "Print and paper are excellent". Heisenberg had offered a ham-fisted theory of the new atomic phenomena and after Pauli had reviewed it, Heisenberg wrote to him: "But why do you have to beat it with so thick a stick?" Pauli wrote back saying all the atomic theories were bad but Heisenberg's was the worst. But Pauli's most devastating critiques came to those who hadn't understood the basic the problem under discussion. To these he would say: "That's not even wrong."

The moral for us is that we should not be afraid of being wrong. Being wrong is a good thing. In that spirit perhaps we can open up our files and begin to discuss with each other, without a fear of being wrong, what our clinical experience tells us about sexuality and attachment.

References

Bowlby, J. (1985). *Attachment and Loss. Volume 2, Separation: Anxiety and Anger.* London: Hogarth.

Davies, J. M, (1998). Between disclosure and foreclosure of erotic transference–countertransference: can psychoanalysis find a place for adult sexuality? *Psychoanalytic Dialogues, 8:* 747–768, 805–825.

Dinnerstein, D. (1976). *The Mermaid and the Minotaur: Sexual Arrangements and Human Malaise.* New York: Harper and Row.

Eichenbaum, L., & Orbach, S. (1983). *What Do Women Want?* London: Michael Joseph.

Fairbairn, W. R. D. (1946)[1952]. Object-relationships and dynamic structure. In: W. R. D. Fairbairn (Ed.), *Psychoanalytic Studies of the Personality* (pp. 137–151). London: Routledge.

Kernberg, O. F. (1991). Aggression and love in the relationship of the couple. *Journal of the American Psychoanalytic Association, 39:* 45–70.

Laschinger, B., Purnell, C., Schwartz, J., White, K., & Wingfield, R. (2004). Sexuality and attachment from a clinical point of view. *Attachment and Human Development, 6:* 151–164.

Mitchell, S. (1988). *Relational Concepts in Psychoanalysis.* Cambridge, MA: Harvard University Press.

Orbach, S. (1999). The vampire Casanova. In: *The Impossibility of Sex* (pp. 7–33). London: Penguin.

Orbach, S. (2004). What can we learn from the therapist's body? *Attachment and Human Development, 6:* 141–150.

Reik, T. (1948). *Listening with the Third Ear.* New York: Farrar, Straus.

Stoller, R. (1979). *Sexual Excitement. Dynamics of Erotic Life.* New York: Pantheon.

Sweetnam, A. (1999). Sexual sensations and gender experience. *Psychoanalytic Dialogues, 9:* 327–348.

The John Bowlby Memorial Lecture 2004

The times we sizzle, and the times we sigh: the multiple erotics of arousal, anticipation, and release

Jody Messler Davies

Introduction

Usually when I begin a paper, I turn to the psychoanalytic literature. I begin to read the classic papers; I turn to Freud, Winnicott, Racker, Fairbairn, Loewald; those whose work has always spoken to me, enlightened me, stimulated my own thinking. I begin to read papers by my favourite contemporary authors as well; those who have already tackled a piece of my current subject of interest, those whose work I particularly respect. But my ongoing love affair with the complexities, textures, and endless shadings of psychoanalytic thought and writing seems always to leave me vaguely dissatisfied when it comes to understanding on the deepest level the intricacies, nuances, and textures of romance, erotic attachment, and desire. (my own as well.) What makes someone "fall in love?" Indeed what does that mean? What do we mean when we speak of "the sexual", "the erotic", "the romantic"? Are they all the same? What are the differences among them? Why does some sexual passion and intimacy grow and elaborate itself in erotic fantasy and play, while some falls flat and dies. Can sexual passion last? Can trust and intimacy survive inevitable disappointments? Can we continue to yearn year after year for the same body, can we continue to turn, year after year, to the same person to fulfil our emotional, physical, and spiritual needs?

The subject itself seems to elude any kind of linear understanding. It is somehow irreducible, deeply incomprehensible, and, at its very core, counter-intuitive. Perhaps it has to be, but I am not sure. It should therefore be of little surprise to me, or to anyone else, that as I began this particular paper, I turned not to the psychoanalysts but to the true experts in this matter, I turned to the great poets. I wanted to see what they had to say about what makes us love, what makes us burn, what makes us desire.

I ask you to listen in with me for a moment:

Homer:

Aphrodite spoke and loosened from her bosom the embroidered girdle of many colours, into which all her allurements were fashioned. In it was love and in it desire and in it blandishing persuasion which steals the mind. [*The Iliad, Book XIV*, p. 214]

Euripides:

Love distils desire upon the eyes,
Love brings bewitching grace into the heart
Of those he would destroy.
I pray that love may never come to me with murderous intent,
In rhythms measureless and wild.
Not fire nor stars have stronger bolts than those of Aphrodite.
[*Hippolytus, I*, p. 525]

Hesiod:

From their eyelids as they glanced, dripped love
[*The Theogony, 1*, p. 910]

Shakespeare:

The lunatic, the lover and the poet,
Are of imagination all compact
[*A Midsummer Night's Dream*]

Dryden:

The pains of love be sweeter far,
Than all the other pleasures are.

[*Ah, how sweet it is to love*]

From these selections we are drawn to the extraordinary singularity of passionate romantic love. We drip, we yearn, we are bewitched. Romantic passion as ecstatic, creative, transformative. Our eyes open into our souls and expose our desires, and our exquisite vulnerabilities. But desire is also inextricably linked with pain. Love holds murderous intent and steals the minds of those who fall under its spell. Otherwise sane lovers are driven to murderous crimes of passion or intensely masochistic acts of symbolic self immolation in order to recapture the intoxicating experience of mutual romantic idealization, or to avenge and therefore survive otherwise intolerable moments of humiliating and unanticipated rejection by those adored others around whom their lives have been organized. If abandonment is the dangerous counterpoint challenging secure attachment, then surely shame and the humiliation of unrequited love serve the same function *vis à vis* romantic love. None the less, despite our apparent understanding of love's unparalleled dangers, the basic human truth emerges. We are, most of us, addicted to love. We enter its theatre with our eyes wide open, and yet most of us enter regardless, craving its intoxicating effects. Romantic passion emerges as the apotheosis of human existence, and our surrender to those unparalleled dangers of wild romantic passion and to the idealized others who steal our hearts and bemuse our minds emerges for many of us as the pivotal moments that mark our lives, organize our memories, and construct its assigned meanings.

Psychoanalysis, romantic passion, and sexuality

Psychoanalysis seems of late, to be undertaking a renewed attempt to untangle and deconstruct the hauntingly elusive structures of romantic passion. Yet, as I read my colleagues, I am struck, as I was when I read the poets, that two loves seem to be emerging; two profoundly different, yet inextricably synergistic strains to the love songs we sing and have had sung to us. We might imagine these strains for the moment as the erotics of darkness and the erotics of light, and they evoke for many of us very different trains of thought in the psychoanalytic literature. When I think of the erotics of lightness I call to mind George Klein's attempt to separate out the tender and sensual dimensions of erotic life; Emmanuel Ghent's (1990) description of "surrender," Stephen Mitchell's (2002) emphasis on the need to tolerate uncertainty and unpredictability if one is to sustain passionate engagement and intimacy; Virginia Goldner's (2004) focus on rupture and repair across the life cycle as the essence of intimacy and romantic constancy; and, most recently, Jonathan Slavin's (2004) emphasis on what he calls "innocent sexuality", a sexuality that exists prior to and alongside the more perverse power dimensions that can corrupt and distort love into something less than.

Dramatically different in tone and texture is the literature that I think of as darker, more ominous, more pessimistic. I think of Sheldon Bach's and Otto Kernberg's (1991) work on perversion as an instinctual preponderance of hatred. Of Kernberg's well known claim that "perversity is the recruitment of love in the service of aggression". Of Michael Bader's ideas about what he terms "adaptive sadomasochism", as representing a necessary aspect of psychological growth. I think more playfully of Muriel Dimen's recent (2005) work on what she calls the "Ewwww" factor in sexuality, the incorporation of physical acts that revolt, disgust, and shame us. I think of Ruth Stein's emphasis on the "otherness" of the lover, and her evocation of Bataille's vision of orgasm as a "little death", in Bataille's terms referring to the "fusion of separate objects and the dissolution of the self". And, of course, I think of Jessica Benjamin's work on recognition and negation; her belief that "what makes sexuality erotic is the survival of the other throughout the exercise of power; the capacity for eros to play with rather than to be extinguished by the destruction wrought by fantasy" (1995, p. 206). These lists are impressionistic and incomplete, but I believe that their inherent differences in emphasis capture something about the nature of my dilemma.

Which sexuality am I to write about? Shall I write about the lightness or the darkness, about cool summer nights, long flowing negligées, roses, fine wines and Shakespearean sonnets, or about dark, hot nights, foreign drumbeats, the pleasures inherent in certain kinds of pain, and the haunting evocativeness of little black leather things. Shall I write about "good sex" or "bad sex", I wonder? In struggling with this I remind myself that "good sex" isn't always so good, and "bad sex" is often much better. But then again, who among us would proceed entirely without those red wines and sonnets?

My clinical work with Rose

Rose was seventy-five years old when she came to me for an intensive psychoanalysis. She was for many years a professor of English at a prestigious mid-western liberal arts college. She was married for forty-five years to Bob, a fellow professor, and together they had three children, now grown. Rose has been widowed for ten years. She is in a new relationship, the first since her husband's death, with Sam, also seventy-five. She tells me rather early in our first session, in a forthright manner I will come to know and enjoy, that she has just experienced her first orgasm and it has thrown her for a loop. "I can't stop thinking about sex," she tells me almost in a whisper. " I want it all the time." "After all these years I thought I knew and understood myself pretty well. But now I just don't know who I am. I have all of these thoughts I never would have imagined. I even masturbate" (she blushes). "I've never done that before. And . . . well . . ." (she hesitates here) "Sam even bought me a vibrator for my birthday. A vibrator! Can you imagine? For my birthday!!! Bob used to buy me sweaters . . ."

I stare at Rose with some surprise. She is, after all, only slightly younger than my own mother. As my whole oedipal structure comes crashing down around my ears, I notice how Rose's tired eyes are glowing with excitement. How the wisdom of her years, combined with the urgency and excitement of her self-discoveries and forthright self-revelations are contagious. I notice also that her thin, papery, ageing skin seems to be alight from inside; a warm, rosy, hot glow that literally strips away the years. She is leaning forward in her chair, eager to share, eager to confide, eager to learn, in this moment she is a young girl in love.

"Do you think you can help me?" she asks early in the session.

"I don't know Rose," I answer honestly. "I'm not even sure yet exactly what the problem is. But I would certainly like to help you understand what has happened to you that makes you feel so unsteady."

"They tell me you are interested in sex," she tells me. "I'm not exactly sure what that means."

"I'm not sure either, but what did you think when you heard that?" I asked her, deciding to make an early exploratory foray into Rose's ability to work with fantasy in the transference.

"I wasn't sure," she giggles. "Maybe you are a sex maniac like me." She is laughing, but clearly embarrassed and perhaps worried.

"Two sex maniacs, that would make us quite a pair," I respond, smiling; choosing to keep the new transference fantasy space open.

"It certainly would. Could be dangerous," she says, her eyes narrowing. I sense her playfulness here. But also a seriousness of purpose behind how she plays. She seems older. Her wisdom reappears. She is searching my eyes for something, staring into them keenly. Suddenly I am the little girl, sitting in my English professor's office. I am being evaluated and sized up. I am aware that I want her to like me . . .

"Answer one question," she says to me; and I know the one question will be a doozey. "Do you think you understand love and passion?"

I answer her almost reflexively. Aware that I am already drawn into a powerful countertransferential wish to be respected and admired by this woman, who has chosen to spend the final phase of her life in such complex and personally uncharted waters. "No, not in the least," I tell her. "I've thought about it, I've written on the subject, I even teach classes about it. But no. I don't really understand it. I think I understand some things, and I'm struggling with others, but the complexity always overwhelms me." I fear in this moment that my insecurity on the subject has dissuaded her.

"Hmmm . . ." she utters, and I sense that she has just determined my final grade for the semester—I fear that it isn't good. "I'm going to give you a chance," she declares. I breathe a sigh of relief. "I'll work with you for a while and we'll see how it goes. I hate people who know all the answers. Damn near impossible to learn anything around someone like that."

I feel that I have just been tentatively hired as Professor Rose's special research assistant, with the security of my workstudy job dependent on the quality of my performance as it emerges over the semester. But just as I begin to take stock of and contemplate the significance of this unique transference–counter-transference paradigm, the particular qualities of the self/other experience begin to shift back again; Rose becomes softer, more questioning, more unsure of herself, more yearning. She leans forward again, and my own authority seems resurrected. She is once again the young girl in love, but also an elderly woman in what are probably the final years of her life, choosing to spend those years hanging off the edge of the world as she has known it thus far. "You know I loved my husband more than I have ever loved anyone.

I loved him deeply," she confides. "But Sam is in my body in a way
that Bob never was. And I have no idea how he got in there . . . I'm not
even sure I love him . . . or am in love with him. I just don't know
anything . . . Except sex . . . I want to have sex . . . with Sam . . . All the
time. And you know what's even stranger? I sense Sam feels the same
way about me. Can you imagine?" Rose is crying now.

As she exits my office for the first time I am struck by how many sides
of herself Rose has revealed to me, and how many sides of me have
been mobilized and evoked in response. I am struck by the juxtaposi-
tion of courage and conventionality, of complacency and a spirit of
adventure, of intimate but domesticated sexuality alongside a passion
that feels wild and new and more than a bit reckless and out of control.
I admire Rose immediately. I am aware that I want to protect her. I
want to make her adventure a safe one, but I am aware that the notion
of a safe sexual adventure is something of an oxymoron. As I ready
myself to shift gears and greet my next patient I hear a lingering phrase
. . . and I am aware, for the first time, that Rose has repeated the
phrase . . . "Can you imagine?" at least three times in this initial session.
As I close the door behind her I find myself wondering, will I become
Rose's Bob or will I be her Sam?

Theoretical discussion

I will return to Rose in the remainder of this paper, as I try and
struggle with some of the contradictions between the lightness and
the darkness I have described, between "good sex" and "bad sex".
I will struggle with the agonies and ecstasies of romantic passion as
described by the poets, with what Susie Orbach (1999) has termed
"the impossibility of sex", with the peculiar sense of dread and foreboding that can accompany one's experience of "falling in love",
indeed, with the very equation of love with "falling", with the
frequent and maddeningly uncooperative struggle between desire
and love, "I loved Bob, but Sam is in my body". I will also struggle
with the polymorphous playfulness of all sexual fantasy—the dark
side of eros—and suggest that its controversial "perversity" and the
shame that often accompanies it are a part of the human sexual
condition. To the extent that we embody our sexualities we are all
perverse. Indeed, the ability to absorb that shame and tolerate it
while extracting sexual pleasure from the very fantasy that has

caused it is a developmental achievement that I see as a precondition for sexual satisfaction.

Ultimately, I will suggest that erotic desire and romantic passion
are inherently disruptive and disorganizing because their satisfaction derives from a complex choreography of contradictory infantile self-states; self–other organizations whose bodily dimension
contains physiological arousal patterns that are developmentally
incomprehensible, deeply disjunctive, and yet, indelibly set. Along
with Joyce McDougall I, too, believe that all infantile sexuality is
inherently traumatic, not because (as she believes) the sexual drives
come into contact with external realities and constraints, but
because, to my own way of thinking, both the cognitive schemas
and the evolution of self–other relatedness that would be necessary
to encode sexual arousal in a meaningful way exists well beyond
the developmental capacities available at the time that early erotic
experience begins.

Sexuality, it seems to me, is unique from the "getgo", and its
satisfaction in our earliest object relationships is different from any
other form of nourishing, interpersonal experience. I ask you to
engage in a brief experiment with me. I ask you all to close your
eyes and hold the experience of eating the most delicious food you
can imagine. I suspect for most of you a just noticeable escalation
of salivation and an experience of deep satisfaction and pleasure
has been experienced. A moment of satiation and fullness. I now
ask you to switch gears completely, keep your eyes closed, and
imagine, if you will, the most delicious experience of sexual passion
and excitement that you can, a memory or a fantasy—it doesn't
matter. Here I imagine no complete satisfaction or fullness, but a
precariously held balance, the holding of a very fine line between
a kind of deeply felt physical yearning and the illusively hovering
promise of total relief and release from its delightfully tormenting
thrall. The point, of course, is that an optimal degree of sexual frustration is an absolutely necessary and irreducible dimension of
sexual excitement and pleasure. The pleasure, in fact, is predicated
on actual enjoyment of the frustration, of being able to tolerate
mounting bodily arousal, excitement, and tension without any
guarantee of immediate satisfaction and release. This idea is not
a new one. Otto Kernberg (1991), building on Fairbairn, sees the
search for "mature love" as the individual's struggle to unite

the exciting and the gratifying early maternal imagos. Muriel Dimen (1999) takes this particularly unique quality of sexuality the farthest in her distinction between libido and lust. Dimen says, "If libido marks the ultimately straight and narrow of biology, lust marks the contradictions, the twinned joy and suffering of the psyche" (p. 425), and later in the same paper, "Two states ordinarily thought of as mutually exclusive—desire and satisfaction, or tension and release—in fact coexist in lust" (p. 431).

My own interest, in the present paper, is to attempt an understanding of the particular object relational implications of this unique aspect of sexual experience, along with its very particular developmental trajectory. I will go on to elaborate this model and suggest that, in fact, two different interacting but separate subsystems of erotic fantasy, in conjunction with very different self–other configurations, take shape in the moments defined by experiences of sexual arousal and yearning and those of satisfaction, pleasure, and release. I will suggest that these subsystems defy integration and remain split apart for a longer period than is typical in other developmental arenas; emerging and elaborating themselves over time, taking on different dimensions within different developmental epochs, and coming together only later and with some internal struggle.

Although I resonate deeply with Dimen's definition of "lust", I would like to amend it somewhat in this context, and suggest that the capacity for sexual satisfaction resides squarely in an individual's capacity to sustain a state of increasingly intense sexual excitement (essentially a form of frustration) along with the equally pleasurable anticipation of its ultimate satisfaction. In actual sexual encounter, or in early erotic experience, the frustration and satisfaction are not entirely simultaneous. It is the affect state I will call "pleasurable anticipation" that holds the intensifying arousal and excitement, making it tolerable, even enjoyable, only because it also holds in mind a belief in ultimate sexual satisfaction and release. In essence, I am elaborating on Fairbairn's (1952) notion that the exciting object was split off from the bad object, and suggesting that the "exciting object" actually exists in a dissociatively split relationship to both the good and the bad objects. I am suggesting here that the capacity for "pleasurable anticipation" represents a developmental achievement in and of itself; the creation of a psychic bridge between an individual's relationship to an "exciting good object" and an "exciting bad object". It is a developmental achievement that allows for the simultaneous psychic coexistence of these two very different self–other configurations and systems of identification and counter-identification, and that allows sexuality to unfold and elaborate itself. A developmental achievement that rests precariously on the capacity to bridge a fault-line of early infantile dissociated self–other configurations and systems of erotic fantasy elaboration. Let me elaborate.

As we all know, cycles of arousal and quiescence begin in the earliest days of infancy. Physiological pleasure is undifferentiated. It builds and peaks and resolves itself only to mount again and again and again. Endless cycles of need and satisfaction whose ultimate resolution is dependent upon the sensitive enough ministrations of a caring and empathic other. As I have heard Beatrice Beebe say on many occasions, the interaction between mother and baby is an erotic dance. My point of course, is that it is in these very early cycles of arousal and soothing that a child's capacity to believe in and rely upon the ultimate satisfaction of intense need states begins to coalesce. Her later ability to hold and actually extract pleasure from frustration and/or arousal, while at the same time anticipating its resolution, begins to form a physiologically-based substrate to the capacity for later erotic pleasure.

I am suggesting that from the earliest days of life and throughout childhood, one aspect of self begins to form and organize in relationship to an object who brings sensual pleasures, erotic tenderness, intimate murmurings, as well as release from the tortures of intense sexual arousal. This is the object into whose arms we fall and melt and merge. We might call this the "good exciting object". This is the object with whom we experience pleasure, cohesion, satiation, a sense of fullness and completeness; as development proceeds it becomes the site of romance, mutual adoration, and mutual oedipal idealization (Davies, 1998, 2003); "love distils desire upon the eyes"; it brings "bewitching grace into the heart", our eyelids "drip love". This is the self–object state in which we stare deeply into the eyes of our beloved; it is the scene of erotic merger and ultimate orgasmic surrender. And yet its survival is precarious. It must somehow be protected from the aggression spilling over in our relationship to what we might consider to be "the bad exciting object", the object who arouses us and arouses us and arouses us. The object responsible for increasingly intense arousal states. The object who teases, tortures, and holds us captive to ultimate release.

"Perversion" with a small "p" and dissociative processes

Across the dissociative chasm, in these emergent self-states of intense desire, yearning, and arousal lie the erotic fantasies constructed to hold and sustain this particularly challenging self–other configuration. These are the fantasies commonly associated with what I have termed the "darker side" of eros, or what we have come to think of as "the perverse", with a small "p". Let me pause here for a moment to elaborate that I am using the controversial term "perversion", always in inverted commas in this paper, to denote a kind of universal, polymorphously powerful, almost always shame-riddled aspect of human sexual imagination; an aspect of sexual fantasy and behaviour that may be experienced as deviant but that, to my own way of thinking and implicit in the thesis of this paper, is anything but deviant. These are the fantasies we think of as "a little dirtier", "a little rougher", and often, "a little hotter". These are the fantasies that we all have and of which we are all ashamed to speak. "I pray that love may never come to me with murderous intent, / In rhythms measureless and wild."

These are the fantasies that involve aggression, shame, domination, and submission, the power dimensions of who loves who more, who needs who more, the will-he-come, the will-she-stay, the must-I-tie-her-up, him-down, in order to hold, arouse, titillate, and drive to distraction and surrender. These are the fantasies that unite the self with a taunting, teasing, ever alluring, "bad exciting object". Indeed one might suggest that an individual's history of playful perversion in fact holds his relationship to this exciting and elusive other. In fact we might consider that to NOT have such fantasies is more pathological than the having of them, since their absence would denote the continued dissociation into adulthood of a system of erotic sexual elaboration that is developmentally inescapable. However, the capacity to sustain this aspect of self–other experience and ultimately integrate it into one's mature sexuality involves the slow metabolization via both fantasy and interpersonal relationship of its intensely shame-riddled aspects; an integration into something more playful, less toxic, less incompatible with pleasure.

Of course, implicit in these separate, dissociated systems of erotic fantasy are deeply held, also dissociated, convictions about oneself as an object in passionate encounters. The self as seen and experienced through the eyes and body and, ultimately, mind of the other. Experiences of oneself as adored, idealized, beloved, sexually attractive, potent, and powerful; fantasies of oneself as a seductor or seductress, some successful and some not; experiences of oneself as a loser of romantic adventures, unattractive, impotent, rejected, and undesirable. Fantasies of oneself as a part object or body part float in and out of our relatedness to others as well, the self as breast, penis, vagina, or anus; the self as skin, mouth, hair; the self as rough or smooth, hard or soft . . . the "how I am used—how I am experienced" dimension of part object erotic encounter.

And so I am suggesting that, for a "developmental while", each self-state and its accompanying erotic world lives independently unaware of the others, split off and dissociated, engaged with its own unique fantasies and imagined object relationships. Integration is beyond developmental ability. The two self-states and their related systems of fantasy coexist, each unaware of the presence of the other. And so our earliest experiences and fantasies of erotic self with erotic other involve two separate and deeply disjunctive sets of ideas, affects, and bodily sensations. In order to protect the good, sensual, gratifying other of idealized romantic merger, tender sensuality, and satiation, a defensive dissociation of self–other configurations is called into play. Not only does the self experience and object experience become primitively split in two, but indeed the entire contents of the erotic fantasy life becomes split and dissociated as well. Clean sex and dirty sex, romantic sex and hot sex, glorious passion and shame-filled eroticism forever cast this primitively bifurcated shadow on all later romantic and passionate encounters and infuse its self and object representations with accompanying fantasy-congruent textures and hues. The question, "Who am I when I stand naked before my lover?" takes on increasing complexity and inherent contradiction. My dilemma about which sex I shall address begins to make sense.

Somehow the developing child and young adult must evolve the capacity to bridge these two dissociated systems of erotic self–other organization, to allow them to coexist, to modulate and contain each other. The experience of a robust and resilient eroticism depends upon their simultaneous coexistence in awareness and their playful interpenetration in both erotic fantasy and actual sexual behaviour. (Compare with neutralization.) The child's attachment base, her capacity to believe in the reliability of her good objects to soothe and comfort, must permit her the psychic space to enjoy the pleasurable anticipation of sexual release, while all the time containing the frustration of ever-heightening arousal and excitement. The capacity to experience pleasurable anticipation must not be overwhelmed by frustration and rage, nor can its fantasied elaboration be inhibited and potentially shut down by an overly restrictive and primitively bifurcated notion of "goodness". A sense of playful adventure, mischievousness, naughtiness, the capacity to tease and not torture, to allure and not torment, to attract without holding literally captive, begin to emerge in fantasy, both reflecting and constructing the bridge between more primitively dissociated realms. As development of an erotic self proceeds we learn, it is hoped, to continue to draw upon the fantasies that began in these dissociated states, but we no longer live entirely within either to the exclusion of the other. The foreground of one is held clearly against a background of both. The deeply bifurcated, pre-ambivalent, otherwise paranoid–schizoid organization of disparate sexual selves and others, the sexual selves and others of defensively dissociated arousal and satisfaction, are slowly woven together into more complex, more ambivalently held, more depressive-position levels of psychic organization and integration. A fantasy that might lean more heavily in one direction is experienced as part of a whole that is inclusive of all. And, thus, the developing capacity to experience the erotic as drawn out over a lifetime, represents a particularly complex self-regulatory and integrative challenge.

A return to Rose's story

In the early days of our working together Rose tells me of her life with Bob. It is a story of collegiate and domestic passage. Two college professors, their three lovely and loving children and grandchildren; mutual scholarly interests, warmth, tenderness, and deep respect. "Sex was quiet," Rose says, "we cuddled, and stroked and talked and laughed . . . Bob would come, and I would hold him. It was lovely . . . I guess . . . at least I thought so then. It was so much better, so much warmer, so much more loving than the way I grew up. I never questioned it." Rose had been the oldest of three children and the only daughter. Her mother had been severely depressed for most of her childhood and adolescence and Rose had been essentially responsible for the care and upbringing of her two younger brothers. She remembered her mother as cold, unavailable, and unloving. There was almost no physical contact between her and her children. "She would be in bed when we came home from school . . . it looked as if she had been there all day. She'd rarely eat dinner with us." It was usually Rose who fixed dinner and helped her brothers with their homework.

Rose's father was clearly the warmer, more emotionally engaged parent and Rose was clearly his preferred child. However, father was away from home a good deal, ostensibly on business, and when he was at home he and mother had little to do with each other. He made sure that mother's physical and financial needs were met, but they rarely spoke and father usually slept in his den/office at the other side of the house when he was there. But Rose's father adored her, and it was she and not mother who was clearly the object of his adoration and affection when he was home. He always brought her beautiful and exotic gifts when he travelled, and wherever he was he called Rose every single night before she went to bed, his own form of symbolically "tucking her in". However, from mid-childhood on, Rose suspected that her father was romantically involved with some other woman. She had once found the photograph of a smiling, vibrant, and attractive young woman tucked among father's papers, and when she asked the identity of the woman, father grabbed the photograph out of her hands in an uncharacteristically angry way and made her promise never to mention ever having seen the picture to anyone, and never to speak to him of it again. Rose's conscious experience was of jealousy, hating this other woman who took her father away from her and away from home. To Rose, the other woman became a slut, a whore, a receptacle for all the negative projections of an excessive, unrestrained, aggression-laden sexuality. She viewed her own relationship with father as the embodiment of everything pure, tender, loving, and romantic. With much halting shame and embarrassment, Rose confessed to me that she had, soon after the incident related, stolen the picture of this woman and hidden it in her bedroom where it lived from then on, as did the fantasy that Rose could eliminate the presence of this other woman from her life as long as the picture remained hidden. It was to be several years before I would come to understand the powerful and increasingly significant role this picture and this woman came to play in her internal fantasy life. Rose's emotional world with mother was constructed of ice. Father had brought some affection and loving engagement, but the traumatic impact of the picture and father's reaction to it suggested to Rose that his heart was not truly hers. It belonged to some other vibrant, smiling woman, someone who looked happier than Rose herself had ever felt. Somewhere in Rose's mind this other woman became "hot", "too hot". Fire and ice with remarkably little space between them.

Bob, it appeared, brought love and stability into Rose's life. Having lost his own mother at the age of ten, Bob fell madly in love with Rose soon after they met, and permanently installed her into the gaping emotional vacuum left by his now idealized and beloved mother. For Bob, Rose became the incarnation of everything good, loving, warm, nurturing, and solid. Hungry for such romantic idealization and adoration, traumatically ruptured by her discovery of father's secret affair, Rose hungrily absorbed these projections, modelling her behaviour, her relationships, indeed her entire internal fantasy life around them. Indeed, as adolescents, Rose's children often mocked her unimpingable "goodness", by referring to her lovingly as "Santa Rosa". There was little criticism, little bad temper, and almost no expressed anger in this household. Having experienced such a traumatic early loss, Bob clearly feared his aggression, and Rose, was terrified of doing or saying anything that might destroy the "halo" through which Bob viewed her. For Rose it was not a bad compromise. If she had to forego the fire, then at least she never again faced ice. Bob was nothing if not relentlessly warm.

But then Bob died, and with him the emotional and erotic straightjacket of his projections. Rose had to master that abandonment and she did. But life's relentless perversity brought Sam into her world. Sam, who was more mischievous, more adventurous, a bit of a devil. Sam, who was, perhaps, not quite so good or kind a soul. As these two stood naked before each other an entirely different emotional and erotic chemistry of mutual projections and identifications brewed. This was a chemistry that placed Rose on experientially unfamiliar turf. She became frightened, she felt that she did not know herself, she was ashamed of the things she felt in her body and the things she imagined in her mind. She was suspicious of Sam, of what she felt when she was with him. She got angry at him, she was jealous of him, she was never calm, but she craved his presence and his touch, and at the age of seventy-five she found that she was almost always hot.

Rose spent the first phase of her analysis describing her childhood, reliving its emotional deadness and the impenetrable coldness that had enveloped her world. She described the contrast in her life with Bob. And she described the anxiety, guilt, shame, and mystification that infused her erotic life with Sam. Bob was so good, Bob had loved her so dearly, Bob had been so consistently and so lovingly available. How could she feel the intensity she had never felt with Bob, with this new and relatively unknown man in her life? The question and its implicit betrayal of the husband she had loved so long and so well tormented her. What kind of woman was she, she wondered. In the transference I seemed to become Rose's guide, her champion, her advocate. I tried to quell her shame, encourage her fantasies, acknowledge her deep love for Bob as well as its restrictive impact. At first this seemed to help. Rose played with these ideas and she seemed to relax a little, but the guilt and shame she felt in relationship to Sam persisted. "Is it OK," she always asked, "to feel this way, to imagine these things, to want the kinds of sexual experiences I now crave?" My role seemed to get constructed as one who taught, encouraged, reassured, and preserved Rose's inherent goodness. Despite my earlier foreboding, I had in fact become "Bob". Rose and I seemed somewhat stuck. I grew restless.

The development of sexual feelings and erotic fantasy life

As psychoanalysts we might presume that the evolving capacity for such a complexly integrated choreography between the exciting good object and the exciting bad object of eros, along with the elaborate systems of object congruent self-experience, situates itself firmly in the individual's highly elaborated and constantly evolving system of internal sexual fantasy and self-regulatory, meaning-making activity. The capacity to sustain a connection to both of these exciting objects and to the self–other experience they generate depends upon the substitution of fantasy or proto-fantasy for the constant presence and attention of the actual object. Laplanche (1970) has proposed that sexuality proper begins when an otherwise ordinary, non-sexual drive tension, one which has been generating a certain level of tension and arousal, loses its natural object, e.g., losing the breast while still sucking. Laplanche believes that the excitement undergoes a process of what he terms "phantasma-tization", in which the natural object is replaced in its moment of loss with an essentially autoerotic fantasy. It is this substitution of fantasy for the actual presence of the other which represents, for Laplanche, the moment in which sexuality proper is born (see also Benjamin, 1995, Stein, and Fonagy & Target for further elaboration of this point).

However, from my own perspective, erotic fantasy life serves not simply a substitutive function. The fantasies and the imagined object relationships that attend them also represent a self-regulatory struggle to contain intense bodily sensation and create the particu-lar bridge between arousal and release of which I am speaking. It is the space in which "pleasurable anticipation" is born, and the space in which it is elaborated. It is the space in which the individual attempts to organize and understand the meanings inherent in the real and imagined aspects of erotic experience itself. The fantasy becomes a potential bridge between defensively dissociated self-states and primitively bifurcated object representations. Psychic fantasy becomes psychological development and ego elaboration in living process. In essence, the substitute becomes the thing itself.

But sexuality seems somehow to spill out of us and to defy self-regulation and meaning-making in the more usual ways. It is this fact that I believe speaks to the tenacity of the bifurcated eros I have described, and to the likelihood that it will elude reliable integra-tion for a far longer time than the split object relations of, say, hatred or envy. One of the unique aspects of our sexual selves is the way in which we assign meaning to sexual experience, sensation, and relationship from a very early age, with a relative absence of any parental input or containment. In an earlier paper, I have suggested that our children's erotic experiences are, in large measure, the one area of intense emotional and physiological arousal that we as parents do not help them to process and contain. We talk to our children about their rage. We sit with them through temper tantrums; help them contain the physiological experience of rage; give them a word . . . anger . . . to help hold and symbolize it. In giving them a word we universalize and normalize the exper-ience, thus helping them to contain the anxiety that may accom-pany the intense affect. We talk to them about what it is that they are feeling, what interpersonal situations elicited it, what they might ultimately do with the feelings. We do the same with experiences of love, jealousy, and competitiveness. As parents we help our children to understand those intense affective physiological self-states that threaten their psychic equilibrium. In short, we contextualize the feelings within the interpersonal realm and make the experience something safe to feel and safe to talk about.

My point is that, at least within Western cultures, this containing, contextualizing, symbolizing activity rarely occurs around the child's ongoing erotic experience. Although it is commonplace to witness our three- or four- or five-year-old children masturbating, or in other states of sexual arousal, it is indeed rare to engage with them in the kinds of elaborate explanatory conversations we are wont to have around the explication of anger or other intense emotions as described above. We are unable to intervene, to offer explanation or context that would detoxify shame and add a playfully transgressive freedom to internal experience. We grow up then, within our culture, lacking both the language to capture, describe and hold our early erotic experience, but missing also (and perhaps more importantly) an internalized relational context that informs us, even later on, that such shared containment and gradual explication of erotic interpersonal experience is even possible to accomplish, let alone fun to enjoy. However, it is precisely *within* such an interpersonal context that we must revisit and resuscitate our infantile patterns of arousal and desire and indeed, play with them in a way that sustains our erotic engagements.

It is only over time and with increasing developmental sophistication that a fantasy bridge between the eros of darkness and light and its actualization in lived sexual experience can begin to evolve. In such a way, a Loewaldian act of true sublimation, "sublimation (a) is passion transformed", can transcend dissociated realms of experience. In optimal situations both the bifurcated fantasy system and the capacity to hold its extremes within an interpersonal context can finally come together in an erotic synergy. However, where development has failed, for any number of reasons, to allow for such an unfolding, psychoanalysis can offer a transitional space, a space in which shame can be detoxified, the capacity to sustain a state of pleasurable anticipation can be developed, and a playfully transgressive atmosphere between patient and analyst can resuscitate lost self-states and object related experiences, criss-crossing between them, holding them together, experiencing them in isolation and in new and emergent blends of transformative integration. When this occurs, I believe we have an example of sublimation as a relational event, as psychic development in process. However, for such a process to unfold the analyst must often forego, or at least delay, more traditional forms of interpretation in order to engage freely and playfully in her patient's fantasies and self–other schemas. Interpretation causes us to focus, to reflect, to *become conscious*. But in the course of analytic work there is often a tenuous balance between facilitating self awareness and creating a kind of inhibitory *self consciousness*. The balance is a difficult one. It is the space in which psychoanalytic aesthetics replaces psychoanalytic precision as the guiding light of clinical choice. The freedom to play and elaborate and experiment becomes, temporarily, as important or more important than understanding itself.

A relational experience of erotic containment and meaning-making

Sometime around the beginning of the third year of Rose's analysis, something in the nature of our relationship began to shift. Rose seemed more impatient, more dissatisfied, more frustrated with the pace of the work. I wondered if she was sensing my own frustrations and restlessness and reacting to them with her own. But the more I reassured Rose the more angry she became. "You're always so good, so patient," she would cry out. "Don't you ever get angry and frustrated . . . don't you ever just want to scream? You make me crazy sometimes." It seemed as if, finally, Rose was beginning to throw my "Bobness" off her back and squarely into my face.

"So my goodness and my patience makes you angry," I suggested. "You hate it, you hate me, you want to scream and scream and scream at me. I have the sense you want to fight."

"Oh I DO Jody, I want to fight you hard. I want to get down on the floor and pummel you when you sound like that. . . . so proper and sanctimonious . . . I hate it. It's like something sticky and disgusting and suffocating . . . I HAVE to fight it off. But you have to fight back. It has to be a hard fight. I have to make you want to fight me and fight me very hard."

"I have to fight you the way Bob never could, I think, Rose. My anger has to be hard and firm, it has to tolerate your anger and my own as well. I have to be angry and bad along with you. I have to let your anger penetrate me, and my anger penetrate you. I think you want to feel the force of it in your body."

Rose was quiet. She seemed lost in a reverie. At some point her anger joined with sadness and she began to cry. "I would hate it when we got like that . . ." she said softly. "It was always me . . . I would say doesn't this make you angry and doesn't that make you angry . . . And he would smile at me with that same soft scolding smile, and he would say . . . 'Now Rosie . . .' OOOO, I hated that sooooo much!!!!! 'Now Rosie . . .' I was bad and he was good and I had to try and try and try to be better . . . OOOOOOO how I hated hated hated it . . ."

"Come on Rose," I said. "Fight with me. Tell me what you really hate about me. Tell me when you can't stand to listen to me for one more single second and you want to squash my words back into my face and down my throat . . ."

"I have an image of throwing a punch right into the centre of your face . . . oh god Jody.... Oooo I don't really mean that . . . but I have to admit . . ." [a giggle here] ". . . it makes me feel powerful. It kind of sends a thrill through my whole body."

"Sort of like good sex?" I say, a slight question and smile at the end of my voice. . . . She laughs, turns her head to smile at me behind the couch . . . then covers her face. I am about to begin to understand the enactment that has been going on.

"Sometimes Sam and I play fight when we make love," she tells me softly and with much embarrassment. "And sometimes, well sometimes, oh I just can't say it."

"What Rose?"

"Well sometimes when I lose, which isn't always," she hurries to inform me, "well sometimes when I lose, he . . . he . . . well . . . Sam he gives me a little spanking. I mean," and she covers her face with her hands, "it doesn't really hurt or anything . . . but it makes me soooooo hot."

"Well if it doesn't really hurt then hot is good," I suggest to her. "And it's sooo good that good doesn't have to be good for you in the way that it used to be. Good can be a little bad, a little naughty. Sometimes it's more fun to be a bad girl. Sometimes it's sexier." I make the choice here not to interpret what Rose is telling me along more traditional lines. I do not tie her fear of aggression in with her mother's depressions or Bob's vulnerability or the vicissitudes of her own fantasy life. I choose to leave alone her desire for me to be hard, strong, and penetrating along with its transferential implications. This may come at a later time. For the present I choose to hold the two aspects of Rose's erotic experience for her so that she can play with the implications in a more open way with me. I hope that the playing with me might alleviate some of Rose's shame. I try to be a little bit more "her Sam". I hope to help her bridge the two worlds between which she has been caught. I try to provide the relational experience of erotic containment and meaning-making that has been absent from her childhood.

Not long after this session Rose informs me, with much confusion and anguish, that she has been having sexual dreams about the two of us. "Very explicit and erotic," she tells me. But I notice that although she is somewhat embarrassed and surprised by the content of her dreams, she is perhaps not as deeply mortified by them as one might imagine from this otherwise conventional and straightlaced woman. Indeed I notice from behind the couch that she is smiling as she relates them, embarrassed but smiling. We are both shocked to discover that Rose, "Santa Rosa", is actually playing with the utterly new dimension of her homosexual desires. Again, we chose to forego understanding in the moment and play.

"I guess this is a little bit more than you bargained for, huh Rose?" I say.

Rose laughs. Her laugh explodes into a heartfelt peal of pleasure.

"What's so funny?" I ask. "Tell me."

"I just had this image of telling my very uptight and self-righteous midwestern children, that not only did their almost eighty-year-old mother enjoy being occasionally spanked by her sexy new boyfriend, but that at the age of almost eighty she was contemplating becoming a lesbian. Can you just imagine that?" Rose turns around to look at me from the couch. "Wouldn't that be just utterly DELICIOUS?" And Rose literally explodes at this point into a heartfelt, body-based belly laugh, one in which I feel free to join her.

I feel it is important to add, in this context, that Rose's emerging and escalating pleasure in a kind of playful and erotic transgression, a kind of transgression obvious in both the content of her fantasies and in her relationship with me, actually paved the way rather than foreclosed a later but more serious exploration of the homoerotic dimensions of her sexual fantasy life.

It is in the midst of our playfulness that Rose begins to remember aspects of her past that had been previously unavailable to her. She tells me that her father always kept an extensive pornography collection, which Rose would guiltily peruse whenever she cleaned his den. She explained to me how she would look at the pornography and try to replace the face of the woman in the picture, the woman she believed her father to be having an affair with, with the faces in the erotic scenes. "I felt as if I had a relationship with the woman in the picture," she confided in me one day. "I loved her and hated her intensely. She took my father from me. It was her that he looked at and loved and not me. But she looked so alive and warm and happy. So different from my mother. I wanted to be her and not me, so it would be me with my father. I wanted her to be my mother. Sometimes . . ." [this in a whisper] ". . . I think I even wanted to be my father so that I could touch her and feel her warm alive body. She was inside me and I was inside her. And sometimes I was inside my father and I was touching her. I think I would get very excited when I imagined touching her, it would be so hard not to touch myself, I would get hot and flushed and I couldn't breathe. Maybe I did touch myself. But then I would feel disgusting and ashamed. And I started to spend more and more time inside that room . . . with those dirty magazines and with that woman. I've never told a living soul about any of this. You must think I'm disgusting! Somehow I gave it all up when I married Bob. He was so good. I felt that I had to measure up . . . that I had to be worthy of him. I saw it as both my escape and my salvation."

Conclusion

There is so much more that could be said about this clinical material, about its relationship to the bifurcated system of erotic fantasy and self–other representation that I am proposing. But we are out of time. I have, I am sure raised more questions than I have answered. But in the endlessly dense arena of our erotic selves that is, perhaps, all that can be hoped for.

Who am I then, who is Rose, who are you, when each of us faces a lover naked? What age? What gender? What body part? What sexual fantasy, from among many, will come to be enacted between us? What trauma might be re-enacted? Which secret desires will be met and which will be frustrated and go unrealized? How many different selves will we hold, how many will we project and allow to be held by the other? What single sexual act, what one-night stand, what lifelong passion can possibly contain all that potential for erotic desire and potential disappointment and despair? The utter singularity of the moment is captured, beautifully I believe, in a short story by Joyce Carol Oates.

> Or was it, Marianne sometimes wondered, the first significant gaze that passed between her and a man, heavy with erotic meaning, almost intolerably exciting in all that it promised, or hinted at, or threatened—[It was] this gaze, this exchange of looks, that constituted the pinnacle of romance: for she had experienced looks from men that penetrated her to the very marrow of her being, and left her dazed, and baffled, and weak, and in a sense, obliterated. And stricken by the realization that no physical gesture, following such promise, could possibly be equal to it. [1983, p. 24. "Old Budapest", *Kenyon Review*, 5(4): 8–36]

Most of us have come to accept, I believe, that our sexual selves are multiple; we are each, all of us, many different sexualities, we are many different body parts, we are many different fantasies, we are many different relationships. Our sexual selves comprise multiple identifications and counter-identifications emanating from different developmental epochs, organized around developmentally diverse cognitive structures and capacities, interlaced and enmeshed with bodies that grow, elaborate, develop, and then deteriorate over time. And all of this, always, in relationship to others, he/she others who are partial, parental, imaginary and ultimately, although not for an extended period of time, actual sexual partners and lovers. In any given sexual moment we construct ourselves and our lovers out of the vast array of possibilities; a kind of erotic intersubjectivity; not quite me not quite you, not quite inside, not quite outside, always unique to the two lovers involved; all the while intensely exciting, but profoundly disappointing as well. Like Marianne, at the very moment of consummation we celebrate our passion and we mourn our discarded options and lost potential selves. We imagine, we create, and we destroy. And, as in all good play, in the very next moment we begin the process all over again.

All available references can be found in the reading list and references (Appendix One).

Response to Jody Davies

Rachel Wingfield

Thank you so much, Jody. I want to begin by saying that it is very special for the Centre for Attachment-based Psychoanalytic Psychotherapy to have you delivering the Bowlby Memorial Lecture today. You have been a very significant figure for us and your work has been key to developing our own clinical practices and, in particular, our understanding of counter-transference and working with our selves and our feelings in the room. *Treating the Adult Survivors of Child Sexual Abuse: A Psychoanalytic Perspective*, jointly authored by you and Mary Frawley (1994), has been a core text for CAPP students. During my own training it was key to developing my understanding of working with traumatized clients, and I still go back to it now, as I find its insights are as fresh as ever.

Additionally, the ground-breaking papers Jody has contributed to *Psychoanalytic Dialogues* form important core papers for our clinical seminars, and have had a powerful and stirring impact on our students, much as, no doubt, her paper has had today. In particular, Jody's work on exploring the erotic in the consulting room has provided excitement, controversy, and passion in our seminars, so it has felt particularly fitting to have her here talking to us about attachment and sexuality in clinical practice.

Jody's work has been important not only to CAPP, but also to the wider field of relational psychotherapy. It has contributed to a shift in thinking around counter-transference disclosure and what it really means to have two subjects in the consulting room.

Today Jody gave us a paper that bears all the hallmarks of her work: engaging, beautifully written, very interactive, involving our imagination and subjectivity as members of the audience, a two-way process, very much as in relational psychotherapy. I was also struck by the poetic quality of Jody's paper and of how much the poetry of her subject matter was expressed in her lyrical use of language.

Crucially, Jody also brought a very real, alive relationship into the room when she talked to us about her work with her client, Rose. One of the qualities of Jody's work that I admire most is her ability to convey how it feels for her to be in the room with a particular person. It is so refreshing to hear a therapist own her responses to a client in such a direct and open way, with a straightforwardness of language that belies the complexity of response underneath. Jody attunes skilfully to the nuances of Rose's feeling states, her vitality, as we can see particularly beautifully in the examples of her playfulness.

So, what a remarkable woman Rose is, and how significant her connection with Jody feels, with so much possibility for exploration.

This relationship stimulated all sorts of thoughts for me, and engaged me with the wider points Jody is making in her paper.

Jody suggests that our capacity to tolerate frustration is directly linked to our capacity to experience sexual pleasure. This provokes all sorts of questions for me. Is tolerating frustration is the same thing as anticipating pleasure? I am wondering why anticipating or experiencing an increasing intensity of pleasure would be conceived of, or experienced as, frustration? Is that inevitable? Or does the very fact that arousal is experienced as frustration tell us something about that person's own developmental history?

I found the experiment Jody asked us to participate in very interesting. Jody asked us to imagine, in fantasy or memory, an experience of the most delicious sexual passion. I tested this out on some friends and colleagues, male and female, gay and straight. I got a diverse range of responses, a range of experiences: some people imagined giving pleasure to their partner, rather than aiming towards orgasm for themselves; others thought about the moment of orgasm itself, and of feeling fully satisfied. Neither of these imaginings involved that tolerance of frustration Jody described. Some thought about having sex, others about realizing for the first time their desire for someone, and the excitement of that promise of connection.

I query Jody's use of the word frustration. A sustained pleasurable feeling in the body may correspond more to our sexual experience. What about the experience of making love for hours? Exploring, discovering, just experiencing the intensity of "being with" someone with such intimacy and arousal over a period of time, in a way that isn't felt to be an increasing tolerance of frustration. This may be a lot closer to *some* people's experience of delicious sexual passion, though not everybody's.

Being able to *stay with* arousal, not feel overwhelmed by it or have to rush to rid ourselves of it, *is*, I agree, very significant here, and is inevitably linked to early attachment relationships—I'm just not sure if this is same thing as frustration. So, I guess I also query the link to an exciting object as being inevitable here.

In Fairbairn's explanation of the origins of the exciting object; he says that in cases of repetitive dissatisfaction, neglect, or violence the infant internalizes the entire unsatisfactory part of the parental relationship: splits off and is then tantalized, and excited by what he or she feels to be the hope of satisfaction in the bad relationship (Schwartz, 1999).

From my own clinical practice, I recognize Jody's model of sexuality, which links to a Fairbairnian-type exciting object. But I would want to place it within a particular relational context.

In CAPP's study group on attachment and sexuality, we have approached sexuality as a social construction rather than from an essentialist perspective, with an assumption that sex cannot be understood outside of its relational and cultural context. I found myself wondering if the (frustrating) exciting object's inevitability here amounts to reformulating it into a concept rather like a drive, instead of something that emerges from certain early relational experiences. For Fairbairn, there is no "good exciting object": the exciting object derives from split off, bad relational experience. Its nature is to tantalize, it will never satisfy. And I guess this does make sense to me.

Jody describes two different subsystems of sexuality: which *I* would broadly characterize as subject–object (one person), and subject–subject (two-person psychology). One is a little dirtier, a little rougher—a subject and an object—"fantasies which involve aggression, shame, domination and submission".

This sadomasochistic subsystem is undoubtedly part of sexual fantasy and reality in the present, and: Davies and Frawley (1994) demonstrate this eroticization of power difference in their hard-hitting descriptions of clinical work with sexually traumatized clients.

But I wonder if this as an essential core of all sexuality—Jody seems to suggest that if we do not have sadomasochistic fantasies this may be pathological. I agree it might be *unexpected* in this culture. *The Joy of Sex*, for example, the best selling mainstream sex manual, suggests that straight couples experiment with gagging the woman during sex on the grounds that "this is irresistible to most men's rape instincts". Enjoyment in bondage, gagging, and spanking I feel has not so much to do with instinct or drive, or essential erotic self–other configurations, but might tell us something about someone's capacity for intersubjectivity and their relational history.

My thoughts also go to gender and sexuality in the real world. When I thought about Rose's story, I felt it linked significantly to a wider cultural denial and repression of women's sexuality, which has left an enormous legacy. Rose is seventy-five, so grew up between the wars. She has the very traditional model of female sexuality for her time. She has two models of femininity. Good woman, wife and mother, vs bad woman, mistress, whore. This split was very apparent in her own attachment history: her mother as the good asexual woman; vs the mistress and the nameless women in her father's pornography, who are only about sex—no subjectivity. This split between good and bad sex, good and bad women, love in the family vs sex outside, is part of Rose's attachment history and the reality of the culture at the time.

The labels "nymphomaniac" and "promiscuous" were commonly used psychiatric diagnoses at the time. Women who masturbated, or had extra-marital affairs, were often given these labels. In fact, I worked with a client myself who was given the label of nymphomaniac by the Maudsley hospital in the 1960s. The treatment for so-called nymphomaniacs who masturbated then included clitoroidectomies and lobotomies.

So it's not surprising that Rose is shocked and thrown by being given a vibrator at the age of seventy-five. And, it is also not surprising that she has internalized this view of female sexuality as bad and somehow separate from "respectable" life. She loved Bob, her husband, but sexual excitement was not possible. With Sam she says "I'm not sure I love him" but it is possible to enjoy sex, to have orgasms. But with Sam she is also the bad girl who wants to be spanked. I would argue that the notion of the bad girl who needs to be punished for her sexual desire is key to the culture the client grew up within and to her attachment history.

I come across this split between a Bob and a Sam so much in my own practice: clients who cannot experience sexual excitement in the context of being in love, or of being in a relationship. It has to be one or the other. Sexuality is felt to be a little hotter in the context of the exciting object—tantalizing but unavailable, unreachable—betraying, humiliating, withdrawing, inconsistent.

So what is it about love that feels so potentially suffocating of sexual desire?

In Luise Eichenbaum's paper, which she delivered at the Bowlby Memorial Conference in 2000, she argued that transitional space is needed for desire.

Is there a temptation to evoke difference to create that space: the foreign drumbeats that Jody refers to, which seem to imply a distortion that there is something implicitly more sexually exciting about other cultures?

I wonder: is Jody also describing something about the way those who fear merger try to introduce this transitional space by evoking aggression, conflict, or subject–object difference? I also wonder if there is an echo here of the essential link assumed by Kleinians between sexuality and aggression? There may often be a link, but is this inevitable?

How would we understand this in attachment terms? We could think about it as a re-enactment of early insecure attachment patterns: ambivalent, avoidant, or disorganized. An attachment to a bad object. For example, clients with an avoidant attachment pattern reflecting a fear that intimacy would be overwhelming: for some people, when it comes to sex even knowing someone's real name can feel suffocating, let alone experiencing a relationship or love. We might think about this in relation to early experiences of being intruded on, and misattuned to, with early bodily contact perhaps having been about the other's need for touch rather than a response to the infant's desire. It would be interesting to think about the insights from Susie Orbach's paper on touch at last year's conference in relation to this (Orbach, 2004). And of course, sado-masochistic re-enactments are very common for those whose attachment figures were sexually or emotionally abusive.

So, in attachment terms, we think about internal working models and how the capacity for enjoyment, exploration, and play come about as a result of security, of availability, and responsiveness. This capacity for enjoyment arises from a confidence in the promise of repair, not from the threat of rupture.

In a good-enough attachment, there is an experience of intimacy as a relationship between two people, intersubjectivity, rather than a fear that connection with the other's mind and body will lead to "merger" or abandonment.

So, what is sex like in this context of intimacy, when there are two subjects in a relationship?

Being seen, recognized, desired, and passionately loved for who you are? Standing naked before someone who sees you and delights in what they find there, and equally that you look into their eyes and see them present, naked before *you*, and *feel* that desire for who they are.

But intimacy, intersubjectivity, feels potentially overwhelming for clients who have never been seen, or attuned to. A client I am currently working with, who has a history of severe self-harm and inflicting extreme and tortuous experiences on herself, believed herself to be inured to pain and fear. She could not understand her response to the growing feelings of intimacy and warmth between us. She said to me, "But I can handle everything—I'm not afraid of anything—why can't I handle this? I'm a nervous wreck in these sessions." Because she feels present, and feels a connection with me, another presence. "When I'm with you, I feel like I don't want to leave. That's wrong."

Stern and others talk of intersubjectivity as a normal developmental stage, but we must not imagine that this is an easy thing: to recognize: there are other minds out there, that I can't control, or predict, that are different from me, that have their own centre of being, forever separate from my own. This is a process of life-long developmental learning. In a history of insecure attachment this is potentially life-*threatening*: the other's mind is not only separate and different, but this difference is dangerous. And what if I do find someone who can bridge that separation without impinging on who I am? What if we do recognize each other, believe in each other, and I lose you? How will I bear that?

Intimacy then becomes fraught—and seemingly impossible. I'm reminded here of Wendy Cope's very short poem, *Two Cures for Love:*

> 1. Don't see him. Don't phone or write a letter.
> 2. The easy way: get to know him better.

> (Cope 1995)

Really knowing someone, here, would actually cure you of being "in love". Romance and desire depend on *not* knowing the other. Humorous though the poem is intended to be, there is something deeply painful and terrified in what it assumes.

On the other hand, beginning to experience sexuality in the context of intersubjectivity in the consulting room is one of the most intense, exciting, and powerful experiences I have ever had in my clinical work.

With my client Ann, the early years of the therapy were characterized by endless sadomasochistic re-enactments. She had a history of abusive relationships in which she had played both roles. She was aroused by conflict, cruelty, humiliation, flirting was linked to insults—a form of play fighting. She knew how to regulate this kind of arousal and it was her familiar internal working model of relationships. Her fear of being annihilated, intruded on by the other was enormous. There was no opportunity for transitional space to develop between us, no chance for us both to be present as subjects and therefore, be found or seen. The possibility of intimacy opened up only when I found my subjectivity in the room and was able to disentangle from the re-enactments. No more games: me as a real person, who was hurt by and impacted on by her. I was not willing to do this any more—I would no longer be an object.

The feelings of warmth and closeness that then grew between us were at first profoundly threatening to Ann, because she felt love for the first time; but she began to feel safe enough to begin to tolerate wanting, desiring, and to begin to experience feelings of desire between us in the room. For a client who had previously been unable to make eye contact, there was now a session in which she just stared wordlessly into my eyes, which was for her a profoundly erotic experience: she could stay with feeling seen, present, loved, and desiring—two people, separate and connected at the same time. There was now no escape from the fact that she was her own subject experiencing her own desire and I was mine, no way of breaching that separation of two minds except by risking being present, being known, being open. Terrifying, beautiful, profound: as hot and steamy as you could wish; beyond a now moment, one of Stern et al.'s (1998) moments of meeting.

References

Cope, W. (1995). *Two Cures for Love*. London: Faber and Faber.
Davies, J. M., & Frawley, M. G. (1994). *Treating the Adult Survivor of Childhood Sexual Abuse: A Psychoanalytic Perspective*. New York: Basic Books.
Eichenbaum, L. (2004). Women and desire: disruptions in engagement. Presentation at the John Bowlby Memorial Conference, London, 2000, *Psychotherapy and Politics International*, 2(2): 135–145.
Orbach, S. (2004). The body in clinical practice. Part one: There's no such thing as a body, and Part two: When touch comes to therapy. In: K. White (Ed.), *Touch, Attachment and the Body* (pp. 17–47). London: Karnac.
Schwartz, J. (1999). *Cassandra's Daughter: A History of Psychoanalysis in Europe and America*. London: Karnac.
Stern, D., Sander, L. W., Nahum, J. P., Harrison, A. M., Lyons-Ruth, K., Morgan, A. C., Bruschweiller-Stern, N., & Tronick, E. Z. (1998). Non-interpretive mechanisms in psychoanalytic therapy, The "something more" than interpretation. *International Journal of Psycho-Analysis, 79*: 903–911.

The John Bowlby Memorial Conference 2004 reading list and references

Benjamin, J. (1988). *The Bonds of Love: Psychoanalysis, Feminism, & the Problem of Domination*. London: Pantheon.

Benjamin, J. (1991). Father and daughter: identification with difference—a contribution to gender heterodoxy. *Psychoanalytic Dialogues*, 1: 277–299.

Benjamin, J. (1998). *Like Subjects, Love Objects: Essays on Recognition and Sexual Difference*. New Haven, CT: Yale University Press.

Benjamin, J. (1998). *The Shadow of the Other: Intersubjectivity and Gender in Psychoanalysis*. London: Routledge.

Bloom, A. (2003). *Normal: Transsexual CEOS, Cross-dressing Cops and Hermaphrodites with Attitude*. London: Bloomsbury.

Bollas, C. (1992). *Cruising in the Homosexual Arena*. New York: Hill and Wang.

Burch, B. (1993). Gender identities, lesbianism and potential space. *Psychoanalytic Psychology*, 10: 359—375.

Butler, J. (1990). *Gender Trouble: Feminism and the Subversion of Identity*. London: Routledge.

Butler, J. (1993). *Bodies that Matter: On the Discursive Limits of "Sex"*. New York: Routledge.

Butler, J. (1997). *The Psychic Life of Power: Theories in Subjection*. Palo Alto, CA: Stanford University Press.

Cassidy, J., & Shaver, P. R. (Eds.) (1999). *Handbook of Attachment: Theory, Research and Clinical Applications*. New York: The Guildford Press.

Chodorow, N. J. (1994). *Femininities, Masculinities, Sexualities: Freud and Beyond*. Lexington: University Press of Kentucky.

Crespi, L. (1995). Some thoughts on the role of mourning in the development of a positive lesbian identity. In T. Domenici & R. C. Lesser (Eds.), *Disorienting Sexuality*. London: Routledge.

Davies, J. M. (1994). Love in the afternoon: A relational reconsideration of desire and dread in the countertransference. *Psychoanalytic Dialogues 4*: 153–170.

Davies, J. M. (1998). Between disclosure and foreclosure of erotic transference–countertransference: can psychoanalysis find a place for adult sexuality? *Psychoanalytic Dialogues, 8*: 747–768, 805–825.

Davies, J. M. (2003). Falling in love with love: oedipal and post oedipal manifestations of idealisation, mourning and erotic masochism. *Psychoanalytic Dialogues, 13*: 1–27.

Davies, J. M., & Frawley, M. G. (1994). *Treating the Adult Survivor of Childhood Sexual Abuse: A Psychoanalytic Perspective*. New York: Basic Books.

de Lauretis, T. (1994). *The Practice of Love: Lesbian Sexuality and Perverse Desire*. Bloomington: Indiana University Press.

Dean, T., & Lane, C. (Eds.) (2001). *Homosexuality & Psychoanalysis*. Chicago: University of Chicago Press.

Diamond, N., & Marrone, M. (Eds.) (2003). *Attachment and Inter-subjectivity*. London: Whurr.

Dimen, M. (1995). On "our nature": prolegomenon to a relational theory of sexuality. In: T. Domenici & R. C. Lesser (Eds.), *Disorienting Sexuality*. London: Routledge.

Dimen, M. (1999). Between lust and libido: sex, psychoanalysis, and the moment before. *Psychoanalytic Dialogues, 9*: 415–440.

Dimen, M. (2003). *Sexuality, Intimacy, Power*. Hillsdale, NJ: Analytic Press.

Dimen, M. (2005). Sexuality and suffering, or the eew! factor. *Studies in Gender and Sexuality, 6*: 1–18.

Dimen, M., & Goldner, V. (Eds.) (2002). *Gender in Psychoanalytic Space— Between Clinic and Culture*. New York: Other Press.

Domenici, T., & Lesser, R. C. (Eds.) (1995). *Disorienting Sexuality*. London: Routledge.

Doty, M. (1999). *Firebird: A Memoir*. London: HarperCollins.

Downey, J. I., & Friedman, R. C. (2002). *Sexual Orientation and Psychoanalysis*. New York: Columbia University Press.

Eichenbaum, L. (2004). Women and desire: disruptions in engagement. *Psychotherapy and Politics International, 2:* 135–145.

Eichenbaum, L., & Orbach, S. (1987). *Between Women.* Harmondsworth: Penguin.

Fairbairn, W. R. D. (1952). Object-relationships and dynamic structure. In: W. R. D. Fairbairn (Ed.), *Psychoanalytic Studies of the Personality.* London: Routledge.

Fairfield, S., Layton, L., & Stack, C. (Eds.) (2002). *Bringing the Plague: Toward a Postmodern Psychoanalysis.* New York: Other Press.

Fausto-Sterling, A. (2000). *Sexing the Body—Gender Politics and the Construction of Sexuality.* New York: Basic Books.

Foucault, M. (1979). *History of Sexuality. Vol. 1: The Will to Knowledge.* New York: Vintage Press.

Garber, M. (2000). *Bisexuality and the Eroticism of Everyday Life.* London: Routledge.

Ghent, E. (1990). Masochism, submission, surrender: masochism as a perversion of surrender. *Contemporary Psychoanalysis, 26:* 108–135.

Goldner, V. (2003a). Ironic gender/authentic sex. *Studies in Gender and Sexuality, 4:* 113–139.

Goldner, V. (2003b). Attachment and eros: opposed or enthralled? In: *What Happens when Love Lasts? An Exploration of Intimacy and Erotic Life.* International Association for Relational Psychoanalysis and Psychotherapy, Online Colloquium, March 2003 at http://www.iarpp.org

Grosz, E. (1994). *Volatile Bodies: Towards a Corporeal Feminism.* Lexington: Indiana University Press.

Kernberg, O. F. (1991). Aggression and love in the relationship of the couple. *Journal of the American Psychoanalytic Association, 39:* 45–70.

Kimble Wrye, H., & Welles, J. K. (1994). *The Narration of Desire: Erotic Transferences and Countertransferences.* Hillsdale, NJ: Analytic Press.

Laplanche, J. (1989). *New Foundations for Psychoanalysis.* London: Blackwell.

Laschinger, B., Purnell, C., Schwartz, J., White, K., & Wingfield, R. (2004). Sexuality and attachment from a clinical point of view. *Attachment and Human Development, 6:* 151–164.

Layton, L. (2004). *Who's That Girl? Who's That Boy? Clinical Practice Meets Postmodern Gender Theory.* Hillsdale, NJ: Analytic Press.

Lewe, K. (1995). *Psychoanalysis and Male Homosexuality (The Master Work).* Lanham, MD: Jason Aronson.

Magee, M., & Miller, D. (1997). *Lesbian Lives: Psychoanalytic Narratives Old and New.* Hillsdale, NJ: The Analytic Press.

Maguire, M. (1995), Are men really fragile? In: M. Maguire (Ed.), *Men, Women, Passion and Power: Gender Issues in Psychotherapy.* Hove: Brunner-Routledge.

Maguire, M. (2004). *Men, Women, Passion and Power: Gender Issues in Psychotherapy.* Hove: Brunner-Routledge.

Mann, D. (Ed.) (1999). *Erotic Transference and Countertransference: Clinical Practice in Psychotherapy.* London: Routledge.

Maroda, K. (1999). *Seduction, Surrender, and Transformation; Emotional Engagement in the Analytic Process.* Hillside, NJ: Analytic Press.

May, R. (1995). Re-reading Freud on homosexuality. In: T. Domenici & R. C. Lesser (Eds.), *Disorienting Sexuality.* London: Routledge.

Mitchell, S. A. (1988). Sex without drive (theory). In: S. A. Mitchell (Ed.), *Relational Concepts in Psychoanalysis.* Cambridge, MA: Harvard University Press.

Mitchell, S. A. (1996). Gender and sexual orientation in the age of post-modernism: the plight of the perplexed clinician. In: S. Mitchell (Ed.), *Influence and Autonomy in Psychoanalysis.* Hillsdale, NJ: Analytic Press.

Mitchell, S. A. (2003). *Can Love Last? The Fate of Romance Over Time.* New York: Norton.

O'Connor N. and Ryan, J. (1993). *Wild Desires and Mistaken Identities: Lesbianism and Psychoanalysis.* London: Virago.

Orbach, S. (1993). *Hunger Strike.* Harmondsworth: Penguin.

Orbach, S. (1999). *The Impossibility of Sex.* Harmondsworth: Penguin.

Orbach, S. (2002). *On Eating.* Harmondsworth: Penguin.

Orbach, S., & Eichenbaum, L. (1995). From objects to subjects. *British Journal of Psychotherapy.* 12: 89–97.

Orbach, S., & Eichenbaum, L. (2000). *What Do Women Want?* London: HarperCollins.

Pope, K. S., Sonne, J. L., & Holroyd, J. (1993). *Sexual Feelings in Psychotherapy: Explorations for Therapists and Therapists-In-Training.* USA: American Psychological Association (APA).

Queen, C., & Schimel, L. (Eds.) (1997). *Pomosexuals: Challenging Assumptions About Gender and Sexuality.* San Francisco CA: Cleis Press.

Rosiello, F. (2000). *Deepening Intimacy in Psychotherapy: Using the Erotic Transference and Countertransference.* Lanham, MD: Jason Aronson.

Roughgarden, J. (2004). *Evolution's Rainbow: Diversity, Gender, and Sexuality in Nature and People.* Berkeley, CA: University of California Press.

Schwartz, A. E. (1998). *Sexual Subjects: Lesbians, Gender and Psychoanalysis.* New York: Routledge.

Schwartz, J. (1999). *Cassandra's Daughter: A History of Psychoanalysis in Europe and America.* London: Karnac.

Shakespeare, T., Gillespie Sells, K., & Davies, D. (1996). *The Sexual Politics of Disability—Untold Desires.* London: Cassell.

Sinason, V. (Ed.) (2002). *Attachment, Trauma and Multiplicity.* Hove: Brunner-Routledge.

Slavin, J. H., Oxenhandler, N., Seligman, S., Stein, R., & Davies, J. M. (2004). Roundtable: Dialogues on sexuality in development and treatment. *Studies in Gender and Sexuality, 5*: 371–418.

Spector Person, E. (1999). *The Sexual Century.* New Haven, CT: Yale University Press.

Staid, G. (1986). Dracula's women and why men love to hate them. In: G. I. Fogel & F. M. Lane (Eds.), *The Psychology of Men.* NewYork: Basic Books.

Stoller, R. (1984). The *Development of Masculinity and Femininity.* London: Karnac.

Stoller, R. (1994). *Perversion: The Erotic Form of Hatred.* London: Karnac.

Suttie, I. D. (1988). *The Origins of Love and Hate.* London: Free Association Books.

Symington, N. (1996). *The Making of a Psychotherapist.* London: Karnac.

Widlocher, D. (Ed.) (2001). *Infantile Sexuality and Attachment.* New York: Other Press.

Introduction to The Centre for Attachment-based Psychoanalytic Psychotherapy

The Centre for Attachment-based Psychoanalytic Psychotherapy (CAPP) is an organization committed to the development of this particular approach to psychotherapy. It provides a four-year training for psychotherapists and a consultation and referral service.

Attachment-based psychoanalytic psychotherapy has developed on the basis of the growing understanding of the importance of attachment relationships to human growth and development throughout life. This approach to psychotherapy, developing from the relational tradition of psychoanalysis, draws upon psychoanalytic insights and the rapidly growing field of attachment theory.

Understanding psychotherapy within the context of attachment relationships leads to an approach to psychotherapy as a cooperative venture between therapist and client. The aim is to develop a sufficiently secure base to enable the exploration of loss and trauma in the course of development. The therapy is designed to create a safe space in which the client can reflect upon their lived experience, their experience of relationships in the present, and their experience of their relationship with the therapist.

Mourning is vital to the acknowledgement and understanding of the effects of abandonment, loss, abuse, whether emotional, sexual, or physical. The support of an authentic process of mourning forms a central part of the therapeutic work. This is crucial to the development of a sense of self, and the capacity to form and sustain intimate relationships. Both a strong sense of self and good attachment relationships are essential to managing stressful experiences.

The losses and traumas to be addressed in therapy are not confined to a private world or to early life. Groups and society as a whole shape attachment relationships formed by individuals. The experience of loss and abuse as a result of structures and pressures and everyday experiences concerning race, gender, sexuality, class, culture, and disability, together with the complexity of the individual's response, can be worked with in a profound way through attachment-based psychoanalytic psychotherapy.

John Bowlby's original development of attachment theory was promoted primarily by his concern to ensure social recognition for the central importance of attachment and the experience of loss in early development. He was also concerned to strengthen the scientific foundations for psychoanalysis. Since his original work, attachment theory has come to occupy a key position in this fast growing scientific field. Attachment theory provides a crucial link between psychoanalysis, developmental psychology, neurobiology, and the behavioural sciences.

CAPP has drawn on a wide range of approaches including the British object relations tradition, American relational psychoanalysis, theories on the development of the self, and contemporary work on trauma and dissociation to provide a breadth and depth of insight into the structure and dynamics of the internal world. The common themes that run through them all are the importance of unconscious communication, of the transference and the countertransference, of containment and the acceptance of difference, and an emphasis on two-person psychology.

The development of our theoretical base is a dynamic and continuing process. The Centre will continue to adapt and develop in the light of new research, contemporary developments and clinical experience.

Trustees of CAPP

Elaine Arnold
Sir Richard Bowlby (Chair of Trustees)
Susie Orbach
James Sainsbury

Chair of CAPP

Rachel Wingfield

Vice Chair

Emerald Davies

Address

Centre for Attachment-based Psychoanalytic Psychotherapy
The John Bowlby Centre
147 Commercial Street
London E1 6BJ

Tel: 020 247 9101

Email address:
administrator@attachment.org.uk

Website:
www.attachment.org.uk

CAPP is a Registered Charity, No. 1064780/0 and a Company
Limited by guarantee, No. 3272512